A SHEARWATER BOOK

Bounded People, Boundless Lands

Eric T. Freyfogle

Bounded People, Boundless Lands

Envisioning a New Land Ethic

ISLAND PRESS / Shearwater Books
Washington, D.C. • Covelo, California

A Shearwater Book published by Island Press

Copyright © 1998 Island Press

All rights reserved under International and Pan-American Copyright
Conventions. No part of this book may be reproduced in any form or by
any means without permission in writing from the publisher: Island Press,
Suite 300, 1718 Connecticut Avenue, N.W., Washington, D.C. 20009

Shearwater Books is a trademark of
The Center for Resource Economics.

LIBRARY OF CONGRESS CATALOGING-IN-PUBLICATION DATA
Freyfogle, Eric T.
    Bounded people, boundless lands : envisioning a new land ethic /
Eric T. Freyfogle
        p.   cm.
    Includes bibliographical references and index.
    ISBN 1–55963–418–9 (cloth : acid-free paper)
    1. Environmental ethics.   2. Environmental responsibility.
I. Title.
GE42.F74   1998   98–39092
179' .1—dc21   CIP

Printed on recycled, acid-free paper

Manufactured in the United States of America

10   9   8   7   6   5   4   3   2   1

For Luke and Anna

Contents

But whoever is joined with all the living has hope. . . .

ECCLESIASTES

Preface

My family home as I grew up in central Illinois was blessed with an expansive, wooded backyard dominated by hickories, oaks, and wild fruit trees. The yard abutted a small, mature forest—only a handful of acres, I now realize, but at the time an expanse of endless fascination. I often roamed this woods, sometimes just to explore, other times, hatchet in hand, to reenact boyishly the pioneer era. Beyond the woods lay the town's oldest cemetery, little visited then or now and intriguing to a youth unsure of how life fit together with death. Inside the cemetery, the disorder of the woods gave way starkly to regimented rows of rectangular graves.

In one corner of the cemetery, a gathering of stones marked the resting spots of unknown Confederate soldiers—prisoners of war who had died on the trains carrying them north to a prison camp near Chicago. Here, far from home, they made their final connection with the land. Close to these graves lay those of the county's first white settlers, people who had known the land before roads, fences, and plows divided it into usable, human-sized pieces. They were the ones who transformed this county into a place hospitable to human life. They drove out roaming bison, elk, wolves, and bears and brought in their favored animals—cattle, hogs, horses, and chickens—most of them protected by fences and all of them constrained by property boundaries.

Our back property line fronting the woods was regularly overgrown with wild shrubs and volunteer trees, and on many crisp fall afternoons I worked with my father to reestablish the clarity of the line. Why we did so I don't know, but it seemed important to us both at the time. In any case, I took pleasure in chopping down plants and earning praise in the process.

For more than a decade, my path in life took me away from central Illinois, but in time I returned to teach property and environmental law at the University of Illinois. As a property law teacher, I came to dwell on the subject of land boundaries and how they've reflected human culture and in turn helped shape it. Like other landscapes, that of central Illinois is dominated by human-drawn lines, by the ubiquitous fences, roads, property lines, and political borders that have, in many places and in many ways, turned nature's organic whole into a collection of pieces and parts. Lines such as these have profoundly affected the ways people see the land and go about living on it.

At the same time, as a committed community member, I worried more and more about the local land's health and its precarious future. Humans here have pushed the land just as hard as have Americans living elsewhere, and it shows. The land remains fertile and highly productive, yet in subtle ways it is sick and slowly weakening, and its natural beauty is much diminished. Like people elsewhere, people here need to craft better ways of inhabiting the land. They need a clearer sense of the rightful human role in the natural order and what it means to dwell in a place permanently, in an ecologically sound, ethically mature way.

Out of these concerns has come this book. Here, I talk about boundaries on the land and in the human mind; about the long-term goal of conservation policy; about the future of private property ownership in a culture increasingly aware of interconnections among land parcels and landowners; and about the actions people might take to soften social boundaries so that, acting together, they can nourish the land's health and beauty.

A clearer vision of how humans fit together with the rest of nature needs to emerge in the new century. At the same time, conservation policy needs to gain a better sense of where it is heading; it needs a more plainly stated goal, one that blends good science and serious ethical reflection into an appealing portrait of satisfying, enduring life. Just as vital are good processes for getting people together to recognize how their fates are intermingled and how the fate of humankind is linked with that of the land—bottom up processes that engage people as citizens committed to the common good. And from these deliberations needs to emerge a new land ethic, an ethic not just for a single landowner but for a collective people inhabiting and thriving on a naturally boundless land.

In writing this book, I've often thought of my father and of those wonderful fall days years ago, raking leaves and clearing the back line. Here, though, my focus is on the future, and I offer this book, with hope and love, to my two children.

Bounded People, Boundless Lands

Chapter 1

Bounding the Land

L IKE MANY OF Robert Frost's poems, "Mending Wall" is a study in contradiction. Set in rural New England, it is a narrative poem about boundaries and walls, in nature, culture, and the human mind. As the poem opens, spring has arrived in rocky farm country, and with it has come an annual ritual: the mending of the stone wall that divides the narrator's farm from his neighbor's. Choosing a date as they have done before, the two farmers walk their shared wall together, each replacing the stones on his side. While the work proceeds, the narrator muses about the rocky wall, his stern-faced neighbor, and the jumbled ways in which people and land fit together. From the neighbor comes only a single sentence. Twice repeated, it is the line of the poem that has become best known: "Good fences make good neighbors."

American culture has latched on to this proverb, no doubt because it captures so well a number of tendencies and assumptions that seem so sensible. We like fences and erect them often, routinely separating "mine" from "yours." We like to divide land and instinctively think of land as parceled and bounded. Frost, however, didn't mean to endorse this adage outright, and the narrator in "Mending Wall" is intent on challenging it. "Something there is," the narrator says, "that doesn't love a wall, / That wants it down." "The frozen-ground-swell" of winter "spills the upper boulders in the sun; / And makes gaps even two can pass abreast." Nature, it seems, dislikes this stone wall. Freezing and thawing work against it, and so does gravity. Wandering hunters also play a role, knocking down stones to "have the rabbit out of hiding." Then there are the more mysterious forces that seem secretly to pull at stone walls. Elves at work, the narrator speculates, "but it's not elves exactly." However caused, the wall's gaps appear yearly: "No one has seen them made or heard them made, / But at spring mending-time we find them there."

"Something there is that doesn't love a wall, / That wants it down."

"Good fences make good neighbors."

As Frost's narrator relates his tale of labor shared, he argues for his side of this enduring tension. The stone wall has no purpose, he points out. The neighbor's farm "is all pine and I am apple orchard. / My apple trees will never get across / And eat the cones under his pines. . . ." Walls make sense when there are cows, "but here there are no cows." So why do fences make good neighbors? the narrator demands to know—silently asking of himself and of the reader but not, importantly, of his neighbor. "Before I built a wall I'd ask to know / What I was walling in or walling out, / And to whom I was like to give offence."

Throughout the poem, Frost seems tilted toward the narrator's view of things, but the poem takes a turn at the end. It is the tradition-tied neighbor who has the last say. "Good fences make good neighbors," he says again, proud that he has thought of the idea. There the poem ends, and the mending work goes on.

"Mending Wall," one of Frost's classics, raises enduring questions about owning and living on the land. Why are fences and boundaries so attractive, Frost implicitly asks, when nature itself is boundless? How do they reflect the perceptions and values of a particular culture? How have people used them, for good and ill, to shape the land as well as their own lives? "A good poem," American novelist and poet Robert Penn Warren once noted, "drops a stone into the pool of our being, and the ripples spread." In the case of "Mending Wall" the ripples set loose are many, and they spread in various ways—outward across the land, backward into history, and inward, into the reaches of human nature.

Frost is clear on only one point: nature has no need for walls, stone or otherwise. When it comes to human needs, his narrative is less definitive. Cows have a habit of wandering, which means that for cattle owners, at least, walls are a positive good. For hunters, walls are a nuisance, if not a danger; game animals don't respect them, so hunters won't either. Orchard owners, needing no walls, think of their maintenance as mostly aimless work—though Frost's narrator is able to view his labor lightly, as "just another kind of out-door game."

With these points made, Frost has covered the practical aspects of walls: They are useful for some purposes, bothersome for others. As readers we're left to consider why people like walls so much and how walls reflect and shape who people are. Why *do* good fences make good neighbors? Is there something inherently appealing about boundaries? Is there something in a person's ability to witness the land, to grasp it in the mind, to sink roots into it and take responsibility for it, that somehow generates the drive to divide? Nature may need no sharp boundaries, but do people?

In the "good fences" adage, nature is a storehouse of commodities, a collection of discrete parts, not an intermingled whole. An alternative view, expressed by the poem's narrator, displays a willingness to set aside tradition and listen to nature, particularly nature's messages about connectedness and interdependence. As the

questioning narrator sees it, his neighbor's yearning for boundaries reflects a territorial longing that reaches back to the Stone
Age. Indeed, so culturally entrenched is this longing that in the
end the narrator bows to it, never mustering the courage to voice
his doubts.

Implicit in Frost's poem, unmentioned by either farmer, is a
third aspect of this stone wall—its symbolism of communal cooperation, of neighbors identifying a shared goal and working together to achieve it. This tradition thrives in the springtime ritual
of mending, which carries on year after year. Frost never explains
why his narrator ultimately holds his tongue, but the farmer's reti-
cence probably has more to do with the maintenance of communal
bonds than with any pleasure he derives from his "outdoor game."
By respecting the wall-mending tradition, the narrator admits that
he and his neighbor benefit from a peaceful coexistence. Good
neighbors get along, and in getting along they foster the well-
being of the whole.

In giving shape to an especially fine poem, Frost raises lasting
issues about the ways people view and inhabit land. Inherited ways
contrast with a tradition of questioning and novelty. Landowner
independence stands against neighborly cooperation. Boundaries,
on the land and in human nature, are set against the unbounded,
organic whole.

DIVIDING SPRING CREEK

Boundaries and the bounding process have been central elements
of American culture since the first days of settlement. The westward expansion of the country, in fact, was a matter not only of
taming the land but also of dividing and bounding it. Through a
messy process continuing for generations, an interconnected whole
became a collection of parcels and pieces. As they divided nature,
the settlers severed, mentally and sometimes physically, many of
the connections that joined nature's pieces into an organic whole.

They had reasons for doing so, of course. But in time, their boundaries and senses of boundedness would take a heavy toll on the land's health.

A particularly colorful chapter in this story unfolded during the California gold rush as miners combed the state, picks in hand, searching for a minuscule part of the state's natural bounty. To miners, boundaries made sense as a way of focusing entrepreneurial energies and keeping disputes and violence to tolerable levels. As they saw it, land possessed value only if a person could use it or extract something from it. Gold, for example, became valuable once it was removed from the ground and sold at market, and water and lumber held similar value. But the rest of California's complex landscape was merely so much passive scenery. The land was a collection of parts—natural resources—a few of them valuable, most of them not.

In much of California, the valuable parts included the water flows that came tumbling down the mountains. Before settlers could use water in significant quantities, it, too, needed dividing. That task, though, proved far harder than the surveying and division of land, for land didn't move around. Water flowed across the landscape, visibly displaying nature's interconnectedness for anyone who cared to take note. Still, the impulse to divide nature was strong, enough so to overcome practical difficulties. Miners proceeded to divide California's rivers just as they carved up its land, driven by the same fragmented perception of nature and the same utilitarian gauge of value.

In the summer of 1852, a business by the name of A. G. Chauncey & Co. built a sawmill in Shasta County, California. Needing water to power its mill, the company chose a promising site at the mouth of a small stream known as Spring Creek. Since Chauncey & Co. was the first party to claim the stream's water, the entire flow was available for its use. Chauncey planned to sell lumber to the region's many new mining operations. Mining methods of the day needed large quantities of water to crush ore, separate the gold, and wash away wastes. To get water to mining sites, often far from any river, miners built dams, ditches, and flumes, often out of wood. Responding to this demand for lumber, Chauncey's mill thrived from the moment it became operational.

Seven months after Chauncey completed its mill, another enterprise, Spring Creek Water and Mining Co., arrived on the scene. Spring Creek Co. staked out mining sites several miles uphill from Chauncey & Co. and five miles away from the river. To get water to its sites, Spring Creek Co. constructed the usual type of ditches and flumes on Spring Creek, upstream from Chauncey. In October 1853, its work complete, the company opened its new gates and let gravity carry the water out of its natural channel.

Through the winter of 1853–1854, all went well. Spring Creek Co. extended its ditch and flume another mile at a cost of $2,000, and increased its water diversion. By July, however, the looming conflict had become evident. Like many California streams, Spring Creek carried mostly winter rain and snowmelt. Its waters flowed reliably from November through May, but the flow dropped sharply when summer came around. Then, with Spring Creek Co. diverting so much of the stream's flow, Chauncey couldn't operate its mill at full power. The company began to lose money and quickly filed suit, asking the local court to enjoin the upstream diversion as an unlawful interference with its vested water rights.

The controversy on Spring Creek mirrored many other gold-rush conflicts as too many water users scrambled for too little water. Although the lands along Spring Creek were part of the public domain, and therefore under the jurisdiction of the U.S. government, the federal government was far from the hills of California and showed little interest in either asserting or protecting its rights. With the federal government silent, miners and state lawmakers wasted no time in carving up the public's largesse. Their chosen method of allocating water was to give it to the first person who put it to use. They could have allocated the resource in other ways, but priority in time seemed like the best approach: It was the easiest rule to administer, and it matched well the prevailing spirit of competition. No government machinery was needed to acquire or distribute water. Few opportunities for favoritism or public corruption arose. Simply by diverting water and applying it to a beneficial use, a miner acquired a property right in a flow, just as he did when he discovered a valuable mineral deposit and physically marked its bounds.

In the lawsuit over Spring Creek, the first-in-time allocation rule pointed to a clear winner—A. G. Chauncey & Co., which had begun its water use nearly a year before the mining company had. The mining company, however, offered a defense: As a matter of law, it asserted, mining was a preferred economic enterprise, so inherently important that the company's need for water took precedence over that of the sawmill, even when the miners arrived second. The argument was plausible, for the law of California did favor miners over farmers and ranchers when resource-use conflicts arose. But the statute that established that preference was limited to the specific case of miner–farmer conflicts, and the court was unwilling to extend it to different water conflicts. The lumber company was first in time, so Spring Creek Water and Mining Co. would have to end its diversion. On appeal some months later, the Supreme Court of California agreed.

Like most legal cases, the Spring Creek dispute never really got to the bottom of things. The court never dug deeply enough to question the fundamental assumptions that gave shape to the law and the parties' legal claims. No judge or lawyer asked whether nature was merely a collection of commodities, quietly awaiting the human call to serve. No one wondered how human exploitation of the stream might affect other life-forms and the integrity of natural hydrologic cycles. Sitting as they did at opposing courtroom tables, the parties appeared visibly locked in conflict as competing businesses, plaintiff versus defendant. One side would get the water; the other side would not. No one asked whether the parties were in some sense parts of a larger whole, fellow members of a community and owing duties to that community. Was it fair to allocate the entire stream to the first few people to show up? What about other potential users of the stream, such as the prospective miners and ranchers who were at that very moment trekking westward? And might California's people and lands be linked together in inscrutable, ineluctable ways, with the well-being of the parts dependent on the lasting health of the whole?

Although the court in the Spring Creek case didn't take the time to range over the moral and intellectual landscape, the case provided it with a good opportunity to do so. The two economic enterprises, it turns out, were closely linked on the land, however competitive they became in the courtroom. When Spring Creek Co. needed to build its miles of ditches and flumes, it turned to Chauncey & Co. for the lumber. Thus, Chauncey was well aware of the planned diversion of water upstream, and it benefited directly by selling lumber to make that diversion possible. For its part, Spring Creek Co. knew about Chauncey's water need and where its power came from. Chauncey & Co. sawed lumber; Spring Creek Co. used the lumber to extend its water line. Together, the companies prospered.

Spring Creek Co.'s argument in the courtroom, though, wasn't premised on any community of interest. The company didn't propose a fair sharing of the water, nor did it ask the court to arrange a compromise or an accommodation that recognized the beneficial links between the parties. Spring Creek Co. wanted all the water it could use during the summer. As Spring Creek Co.'s lawyers saw it, Chauncey & Co. had implicitly granted Spring Creek Co. license to the water by selling it lumber with full knowledge of its plans for water-diversion. By its actions, that is, Chauncey had given up some of its rights.

On appeal, California's supreme court rejected this implied-license argument, and in doing so, it emphasized the importance of finishing first in the race to seize and divide. In this case and in others like it, the court gave birth to a new set of legal rules governing the allocation of water. The new method, known as prior appropriation, quickly gained converts among lawmakers throughout the arid, frontier West, for it seemed to fit well with both the land and the settlers' temperaments. Except in isolated pockets—in Mormon Utah and the Spanish-speaking Southwest—the ethic of western settlement was predominantly an ethic of individualism and competition. Settlers arrived as individuals and as families and looked after their own. Fairness and good fences they understood. Shared ownership and an unbounded land they did not.

The old common-law scheme of water rights—the scheme that western states largely cast aside—was the riparian rights method of water allocation, in which water rights were part of the bundle of rights held by an owner of waterfront land. Riparian doctrine required a rough sharing of water among all riparian landowners, and no owner could overuse the river to the disadvantage of other owners. To most western settlers, however, that legal scheme made little sense. Much of the West's land was owned by the federal government, and many disputes, such as the one over Spring Creek, arose in settings where neither claimant owned riparian land. Riparian rights were also unappealing because they were so restrictive. Under riparian law, a water right was attached to a piece of waterfront land and was rooted to its watershed of origin. A landowner couldn't divert water outside the watershed or, as Spring Creek Co. did, channel it miles from its natural home. From the beginning, California's miners disliked these restrictions. They wanted water where the mines were, and thus they demanded rights to divert streams in whatever manner and to whatever extent was necessary to maintain their operations. They also wanted secure, protected rights, including the right to drain a river dry if needed, with no obligation to share the resource with people to come later.

By bowing to these demands, the Supreme Court of California added momentum to the American practice of dividing nature into economic commodities and ignoring communal context. Under the new western water law, competitive individualism reached its zenith. Sharing came to an end, or at least the law no longer required it. Watersheds no longer counted. The natural integrity of a waterway became irrelevant.

It is easy, a century and a half later, to criticize life in the mining camps, yet one can just as easily understand what was done and why. Unlike landscape painter Thomas Moran, who captured western landscapes on panoramic canvases, and naturalist John Muir, who roamed the Sierra Nevada in the closing decades of the century, California's miners and early settlers had little time for aesthetics and nature study. They had to find quick ways to make a living, concentrating their labor and avoiding squabbles with neighbors. A utilitarian view of nature helped feed mouths. Dividing the land focused energies and provided incentives to labor, and the new water law gave people a clear sense of what they owned and how their rights stacked up against those of neighbors. By acting as they did, settlers rewarded the industrious among them and encouraged one another to respect boundaries and avoid looking over fences.

For California's early settlers, bounding the land was simply the logical course to follow. The national economy pushed them to act that way, and so did their inherited intellectual and cultural traditions. Yet once boundaries were drawn, they took on lives of their own. They added legitimacy to extractive practices that soon proved damaging, practices such as draining rivers dry, demolishing mountainsides to get a few pounds of gold, and hoarding resources to the detriment of other community members. Boundaries promoted human supremacy and encouraged settlers to overlook connections and communal links.

Had early California settlers been different people altogether, they might have divided the land in other ways, ways that reflected natural transition zones such as watershed lines and forest-field edges and that encouraged people to recognize their natural and social links. In other words, the problems that arose in California weren't an inevitable consequence of bounding the land. Instead, the problems reflected the choices settlers made as they did their bounding work—what they divided and how they divided it, how rigidly they respected their artificial lines, and how insensitive they remained to the invisible ties that knitted acre to acre, neighbor to neighbor, and people to land.

ECOLOGY AND THE OLD GRID

Not until the rise of ecology at the beginning of the twentieth century did people begin to think seriously of land as a natural system with interconnecting parts. A century earlier, Thomas Jefferson had vigorously promoted an orderly division of the American land, beginning with the Northwest Territory. Surveyors were sent forth to draw rectangular grids on the land, dividing the wilds into counties, townships, and ultimately homesteads, with little concern for terrain or other natural features. That system had its virtues, but in time ecology made the lines appear artificial. As some observers would come to see it, the rectangular grid system caused as much harm as it did good.

Survey lines seemed to tame the land and make it more orderly, but the orderliness was more evident on paper than on the land itself. Activities conducted in one place plainly didn't stay there. Flowing water paid little attention to political boundaries and property lines, which meant that water pollution didn't either. Animals wandered from place to place, and to remain healthy they needed suitable habitat and protection everywhere they roamed. When a farmer installed drainage lines to get rid of rainfall quickly, downstream landowners suffered from flooding and drought. Eroding soil in one place forced people down river to build higher levees. Leaking chemicals on one private parcel reduced waterfowl populations on private lakes hundreds of miles away.

The popular wisdom of ecology—that everything in nature is connected to everything else—contains an element of exaggeration, yet nature's links nonetheless are pervasive, cumulative, and elusive. The closer one looks, the less separation one sees in land parcels and land uses. To an observer attentive to connections, the land appears as more an integrated whole than a collection of distinct pieces, just as Frost's narrator sensed. Landowners and land managers appear not as independent operators, coincidentally working in adjacent spaces, but as co-workers in a larger enterprise, dependent for their individual success not only on their separate work but also on the long-term thriving of that larger enterprise. As readers of Rachel Carson's *Silent Spring* learned to their surprise, minute traces of a toxic compound such as DDT could pass invisibly from organism to organism, accumulating and concentrating as they moved along and spreading geographically to the most remote places on Earth.

When lawmakers began addressing environmental problems in earnest, around 1970, they focused mostly on pollution issues, proclaiming that water pollution would end entirely and that air pollution would soon approach the same goal. Pollution was viewed as a harm that one landowner imposed on another, an evil substance dumped across a boundary without permission. The solution, the law seemed to say, was to pay more respect to the integrity of each land parcel. Landowners simply needed to keep their pollution to themselves. That approach made sense in the pollution context, but problems that stemmed from intensive land uses weren't much helped by it. To halt the disappearance of wildlife and wildlife habitat, for instance, landowners needed to coordinate their land-use practices, not live in isolation. Landscape-level restoration required a more holistic view of nature, one that questioned the grid mentality of Jefferson's age.

One of the challenges facing humankind today—the preeminent one, many think—is to find ways of living that respect nature's wholeness and that account for the needs and moral value of future generations. It is a large, enigmatic challenge, one that deserves our continuing attention and deliberation. To meet this challenge, we need a clearer sense of what right living is all about and what the land requires to remain productive. What might right living mean when put into practice? What does it mean for the land to be fruitful and healthy? To what extent are these questions matters of science and practical utility, and to what extent are they better understood in moral terms? And how, finally, does human ignorance fit into this, particularly the vast limits on human knowledge about nature's intricate ways?

Clearly, the divisions and boundaries that people have drawn on the land need revisiting as part of this effort to promote the land's well-being. For the devoted environmentalist, the temptation is to wipe the land clean of all boundaries, except perhaps those that reflect watershed lines and other natural transition zones. A healthy land, after all, is an organic whole, not a collection of splintered and ecologically unhealthy parts. To a mind focused on that whole, there is much to like in Frost's iconoclastic narrator and much to criticize in California's mining camps. Yet the pursuit of a healthy land must also recognize the realities of human nature. Nature may have no use for walls and boundaries, but humans often do, and the boundary issue becomes complex when people are added to the land. Land management is engaged in by ordinary people— people who inevitably possess limited abilities, people with ingrained values and attitudes, people who usually can know well only a few places and whose love of the land can stretch too thin. For practical-minded people, an unbounded land is no easy thing to grasp.

Whatever its costs, then, bounding of the land has helped people carve successful lives out of the wilderness. Boundaries respond to the market's need for clearly defined assets and for property rights that are sufficiently secure to stimulate energy and investment. Boundaries also play a role in focusing and encouraging an individual landowner's concern for the land and sense of rootedness. Finally, they play a role in promoting a sense of community, which in turn helps foster the land's health. As exemplified in Frost's wall-mending work, shared social traditions are vital to the maintenance of communal harmony. Ultimately, they'll be just as vital to the achievement of a healthy land.

Chapter 2

Taking New Bearings

ONE CONSEQUENCE of the environmental movement of the 1960s was a growing tendency to think of the land as more than a gridlike expanse. People began to realize that nature didn't come divided into regular squares; it wasn't merely a collection of natural resources that a person could seize or buy, move from place to place, and consume at will. The land was more interconnected and intricate than that, and the more it was studied, the less divisible it seemed to be.

The 1960s were a formative time for environmentalism in the United States. When the decade began, environmentalism remained a collection of distinct reform causes, ones that focused largely on particular problems related to resource use and threats to public health, such as timber clear-cutting, wasteful water projects, soil erosion, and declining bird populations. By the end of the 1960s, these narrow causes had given rise to a broader social movement and to an impressive list of victories. For the first time, national forests were governed by multiple-use guidelines. No longer was logging to be their primary focus; instead, the U.S. Department of Agriculture's Forest Service had to pay attention also to recreation, wildlife, and other land uses. In urban areas, too, reformers were changing the environmental landscape with the enactment of long lists of local pollution ordinances and health-inspection requirements. Other environmental victories included the establishment of an array of national parks, passage of the Wilderness Act of 1964, and early national efforts at controlling water and air pollution.

Despite these victories and despite environmentalism's broad base, the movement's critique of modern culture remained vague and in many respects superficial. Environmentalists stood tall and proud on Earth Day 1970, but the movement really had no unifying goal; it was long on criticism yet short on the specifics of how people ought to live and think, day in and day out, as responsible members of the planetary community. Particular environmental campaigns, to be sure, had aims that were easily articulated. Pollution and toxic wastes endangered human health and were readily depicted as threats. Majestic mountains and rivers were aesthetic jewels, worth preserving for their beauty and recreational value. Renewable resources such as timber and wheat satisfied basic human needs; it was obvious folly to degrade the lands that produced them. But stitching particular goals such as these into a coherent fabric proved no easy task.

Was the environmental aim simply to make Earth safer for people and more productive of the things people consumed? Was the goal to craft new, individual rights to a clean environment, along the lines of the various civil liberties enshrined in the Bill of Rights? Or should a healthy environment instead be seen as a type of collective good, an entitlement of communities or even entire generations rather than individuals? Popular slogans referred to "Mother" Earth, but how literally was one to take the metaphor, and what did it mean, practically speaking, to love or obey Mother Earth? Then there was the image of "spaceship" Earth—a metaphor that expressed vividly the precarious nature of all planetary life yet also seemed to cast people as pilots and mechanics, in full control of the planet's destiny. The science of ecology obviously played an important role in all this, and so did economics. But much environmental rhetoric was couched in ethical terms, and it was by no means clear how the pieces all fit together.

As time went on, serious environmentalists began talking and writing more about ultimate goals and how the ethical and ecological aspects of the human predicament ought to fit together. Some of that mental work was done by scholars and writers, but much of it emerged from the activist front, where growing resistance to environmental demands pushed activists to hone their arguments and develop a more forceful sense of direction. Increasingly, environmental rhetoric referred to such broad goals as sustainability and ecological integrity. Criticisms of boundaries expanded from artificial boundaries on the land to boundaries in the human mind, the ones that mentally separated us from nature and that keep us from seeing the land's intricacies. A clearer sense of direction became particularly important as environmental campaigns moved beyond the problems posed by major industrial polluters—problems that involved seemingly bad actors and that everyone could understand—to address issues that were far less obvious and much closer to the lives of ordinary people.

A particularly vivid chapter in environmentalism's intellectual growth took place in the mid-1970s, in a battle that galvanized the attention of people throughout the country. On one side stood the powerful Tennessee Valley Authority, one of the nation's largest land developers and a symbol of economic progress. On the other side was a small band of environmentalists, troubled by the looming loss of yet another free-flowing river. The battle began in little-known Coytee Springs, along the Little Tennessee River in southeastern Tennessee. There, in 1973, a University of Tennessee ichthyologist came across a previously unknown species of perch, *Percina tanasi*. Commonly called the snail darter, the small fish was listed as endangered in 1975 and quickly became the pawn in an ongoing effort to halt the TVA's Tellico Dam, then nearly complete.

The snail darter case proved divisive and confusing, and not just because of the millions of dollars already spent on the reservoir project. Preserving the snail darter simply didn't make sense in terms of the arguments commonly used to justify environmental laws. The fish met no human need for food or fiber. It kept no annoying pests in check, nor did it clean up any human messes. At three inches in length, the darter stirred no fisherman's blood, and its aesthetic value was, at best, modest. The case for preserving the darter was uneasy, and environmentalists were unsure how to present it. Compounding the problem was the reality that environmentalists had opposed the dam even before the darter was found. The darter became central only because the Endangered Species Act protected it: By saving the darter, environmentalists could save the river.

In the end, environmentalists won their lawsuit and the dam was temporarily halted, but they ultimately lost the larger battle. A last-minute legislative deal exempted the Tellico Dam from the Endangered Species Act, and the act was amended to create a new endangered species committee, commonly referred to as the "God Squad," empowered to authorize similar projects despite their harm to imperiled species. Too few citizens, it seemed, understood the arguments in favor of the snail darter; too many considered it the height of lunacy to put an obscure fish ahead of a powerful economic project. For environmental activists, it was a time to regroup and rethink.

The familiar environmental arguments, the ones ordinary people could easily grasp, centered on identifiable, quantifiable benefits that people derive from a productive, clean world. But these arguments applied poorly if at all to controversies such as the snail darter case. The pro-darter arguments were more radical ones, overtly moral and ecological, and their link to human welfare was indirect at best. As a mode of public discourse, environmental thought was taking a turn into less familiar territory.

The questions raised by the Tellico Dam case never received answers that the broader public considered persuasive and coherent. The controversy was resolved, and environmental campaigns mostly returned to more familiar rhetorical terrain. As activists saw things, winning battles was more important than developing well-crafted philosophies. Still, the Tellico Dam case proved pivotal, for it pushed serious environmentalists to reflect on basic questions of value and ethical priorities. It pushed them to think more about where they were heading and how their particular efforts to protect the land fit into both a unified critique of modern culture and a more coherent call for new ways of understanding nature and inhabiting the land. Environmental policy, it had become clear, wasn't just about conserving resources and protecting people from direct threats. It was about other things as well—ecological interconnections, limits on science and human perception, flaws in market processes, the welfare of future generations, the perils of individual autonomy, the moral value of nonhuman life, and many related matters. For environmentalists, the daunting challenge was to bring these pieces together into a message ordinary people could understand.

Environmental thought continues to evolve and mature as controversies erupt over particular places and activities. On the broad environmental front, new ideas are regularly tested against older ways of envisioning, bounding, and valuing the land. Three recent disputes, illustrative of many others, offer evidence of where environmental thought stands at present. In them, one sees in action the basic environmental criticisms of modern culture. Extrapolating from them, one gets a sense of where the path ahead might lead.

Three Scenes

By the summer of 1993, cattle rancher Clayton Williams was ready to do battle. A former candidate for the governorship of Texas, Williams owned a 90,000-acre spread in the rolling, arid sagebrush land of Carbon County, Wyoming, a place where ranching and mining had long held reign. Like many ranchers, Williams disliked Wyoming's long-standing practice of regulating wildlife and hunting on privately owned land. As he saw it, that practice conflicted with the bundle of private rights a landowner held, particularly the landowner's right to control the land and everything that lived there.

Williams was no stranger to the legal process, and he was prepared to defend his rights as he understood them. To press his claim, Williams engaged the legal services of Karen Budd. A conservative lawyer, Budd was well known for her work on the wise-use campaign, which sought to turn back the calendar to the days when extractive activities—mining, irrigating, grazing, and timber harvesting—were the undisputed best uses of the land. In his suit in federal district court, Williams claimed that Wyoming's wildlife regulations amounted to a taking of his private property without payment of just compensation. Landowners, he alleged, possessed an exclusive right to hunt wild animals on their lands. As his complaint put it, the "elk, deer, antelope and other game that lived on or crossed the plaintiffs' land are not the property of the state of Wyoming."

Like many lawsuits, Williams's action reflected a mixture of economic and ideological motives. A victory would bring Williams economic gain by giving him full control over hunting on his land, including the right to sell hunting permits at whatever price and in whatever quantities the market might support. Under state property law, Williams already held substantial rights. He had the right to restrict hunters' access to his land, which meant he could collect fees from those who wanted to hunt there. He could also collect fees from people who needed to cross his land to get to hunting spots on the other side. But Wyoming's wildlife agency made the initial decisions about who and how many could hunt in the state. Williams could therefore invite only hunters with state licenses, a regulatory limit that kept many customers away. Moreover, license fees were paid to the state, not to the private landowner. Williams wanted that system changed. He wanted the power to invite any hunters he chose, and in any numbers he chose, particularly out-of-state hunters willing to pay high fees to visit a well-stocked game ranch.

Prospects for financial gain, however, were probably less important to Williams and other wise-use advocates than was their wide-spread frustration over the growing number of environmental limits on private land. For the wise-use cause, this was a chance to strike back, an opportunity to reassert the ideas of dominion that had prevailed a century earlier, when open frontiers and a culture of individualism bred a sense of landowner freedom. For the wise-use movement, property lines were inviolate. They divided the domain of one owner from another, signaling the end of one management plan and the beginning of the next. They illustrated and implemented the independence not only of landowners but also of the land parcels themselves.

Williams's suit triggered a quick response from many quarters. Fish and game managers complained that wildlife management by individual landowners would lead to overharvesting and to unbalanced, unhealthy ecosystems. Hunting groups and outfitters bemoaned the prospect of new pricing structures, palatable only to the wealthy, that might "take the common hunter completely out of the picture." One editorial in a regional newspaper likened Williams to the kings and land barons of medieval England who reserved hunting rights in Sherwood Forest for the rich and powerful. Environmentalists saw an end to "the concept of free-ranging wildlife, wildlife managed for the future instead of today's marketplace, and natural-resource ownership by the public."

When he filed his suit, Williams probably knew he stood little chance of success. A century earlier, the United States Supreme Court had ringingly endorsed the rule that states own all wildlife. Wild animals, the Court proclaimed, belong to the people in their collective sovereign capacity. States have the power to regulate wildlife as long as they do so "for the benefit of the people, and not as a prerogative for the advantage of the government as distinct from the people, or for the benefit of private individuals as distinguished from public good." Private landowners, then, could hunt animals only to the extent permitted by state law. In 1981, the Colorado Supreme Court had turned aside a challenge nearly identical to Williams's claim. In that case, *Collopy v. Wildlife Commission, Colorado*, a farmer complained when the state banned goose hunting on his land. Even though the geese were damaging the farmer's property, the court rejected his claim that a hunting ban interfered unduly with his landownership rights. "The right to hunt wild game upon one's own land," the court concluded, "is not a property right enforceable against the state."

By filing suit in 1993, Williams added his voice to the public debate on landownership. Before the court of public opinion—the more important tribunal in the long run—he recounted his vision of how humans ought to relate to wild animals. He challenged the rising principles of community and interconnectedness. He sounded a distinct note for land-use rules based on human dominance, minimal government, and individual independence.

The federal judge who heard Williams's case understood its importance. At issue was "the relationship between sovereign and private citizen over one of the oldest and most sacred rights possessed in a democratic society, the right to own and use real property." But the state of Wyoming by statute had long claimed ownership of all wildlife "in its sovereign capacity for the common benefit and interest of all of its citizens." Given this statute, Williams's claim could not stand. The state had extensive power to regulate the wildlife within its borders, enough power to sustain the regulations Williams so disliked.

Taking the case to the federal appellate court, Williams softened his claim, this time asking not for an unlimited right to hunt but merely for the right to hunt his land's "harvestable surplus" of animals—the right, that is, to "the excess animals available for hunting which were produced on the land." But he fared no better with this claim. The appellate court rejected Williams's appeal outright, declaring that the state's wildlife laws did not disrupt his property rights so severely as to amount to an unlawful taking of his property. Williams retained full rights to farm and graze his lands, and he still held the right to exclude people. If his property rights were diminished by the state, the interference was a rather modest one overall, the kind landowners must accept as a reality of life.

WHILE CLAYTON WILLIAMS was pressing his wildlife claims in the arid West, Kevin Proescholdt awaited word from the USDA Forest Service in downtown Minneapolis. As executive director of the Friends of the Boundary Waters Wilderness, Proescholdt for years had pushed the Forest Service to change its management of the Superior National Forest in far northern Minnesota, particularly its management of the million-acre Boundary Waters Canoe Area wilderness. When the Forest Service released its new management plan for the wilderness area, Proescholdt liked much of what he saw. But before the plan could take effect, it needed to withstand a flurry of administrative appeals, and opposition to the plan was strong.

When the Boundary Waters Canoe Area was added to the National Wilderness Preservation System in the 1970s, special rules allowed the continuation of activities banned in other wilderness areas. Motorboats were permitted on many lakes where they had long been used. At several portages, trucks could continue to move visitors and gear from lake to lake. To wilderness purists, these relaxed rules were damaging and inappropriate. Equally disturbing was the damage wrought by the Boundary Waters' growing popularity. Its clear waters, rugged forests, bears, moose, and loons were potent tourist attractions; even the blackflies and mosquitoes didn't keep people away. As the numbers of visitors increased, so did complaints about noise, congestion, and degraded campsites. Portage trails were crowded. Campsites were scarce on late-summer weekends. Seekers of solitude sometimes departed unfulfilled.

The move to protect the Boundary Waters had begun early in the century, after loggers had stripped much of the region of its majestic white pines. By midcentury, cabins and resorts dotted the shores of many lakes in the area, including the sprawling, many-armed Basswood Lake along the Canadian border. Soon, though, the Forest Service agreed that the Boundary Waters might best serve the nation if further development ended and the land was set aside as an ecological and recreational enclave. Protection increased, step by step, until the Boundary Waters achieved full legal wilderness status in 1978. As part of the preservation plan, Congress spent millions of dollars buying and removing cabins and resorts. New physical structures were strictly barred. Even modest facilities for canoeists—picnic tables and canoe rests—were allowed to disintegrate.

Wilderness protection had never enjoyed more than mixed support among the citizens of nearby Ely, Minnesota; establishment of the wilderness area had fueled new jobs serving the canoeing and fishing crowds, but logging and mining jobs had declined. The local mood had soured in the late 1980s, when the Forest Service began to weigh carefully the mounting complaints from visitors who thought the Boundary Waters too noisy and crowded. Kevin Proescholdt and his Minneapolis-based Friends group pushed for more restrictive limits—fewer groups allowed entry, fewer motorboats, and smaller group sizes. It wasn't enough, Proescholdt believed, for the Forest Service to ban mining, timber cutting, cabins, and roads. The appeal of wilderness diminished too much when paddlers had to wait in line to cross portages and had to halt at midday in order to secure decent campsites. Yet fewer entry permits and smaller group sizes inevitably meant fewer visitors to Ely stores and thus limits on the community's economic growth. Worried about the direction in which the Forest Service was heading and annoyed at the influence of outsiders from Minneapolis, various local business owners and civic leaders formed an organization to press their concerns, Conservationists With Common Sense. When the Forest Service finally released its management plan, CWCS was ready. So was Kevin Proescholdt.

The new plan lowered the allowable number of permits for overnight travel by groups. Maximum group size dropped from ten people to nine; more significantly, only three canoes were allowed per party. Motorboat quotas also declined, as did the overall number of authorized campsites. With these and other changes, the Forest Service sought to limit the human presence. Proescholdt didn't get everything he wanted, but he considered the new plan a victory nonetheless.

Within three months, sixteen different appeals to the plan were filed, challenging nearly every provision. As with Clayton Williams's lawsuit, the appeals focused less on economic issues than on competing visions of the link between people and the land. As the Friends saw it, the Boundary Waters was a vast ecological laboratory, a place to study nature's ways and a benchmark for measuring how much people had altered other lands. The area was a refuge not only for moose, wolves, and other animals at risk in unprotected areas but also for the various ecological processes human activities tend to disrupt. Just as vital was the area's value as a spiritual retreat, a place of solitude that was easily disturbed by obvious signs of human presence.

Outfitters in nearby Ely had a different perspective. Although quick to admit the appeal of wilderness—they, too, enjoyed its splendors—they also depended on the wilds to earn a living and were proud to reap the economic benefits of a natural area without having to clear-cut its trees and pollute its waters. New limits on permits and group sizes, they claimed in their appeal, cut into their business with few offsetting benefits. Respecting the land was one thing; leaving it untouched was quite another. It just didn't make sense to place land off limits to even modest human use.

Months later the Forest Service handed down its ruling, upholding the new plan but increasing the maximum allowable number of watercraft from three per group to four, leaving unchanged (at nine) the maximum group size. Not satisfied, Ely outfitters continued pressing their claims, shifting to federal district court. Three years later, after considering the various arguments and visiting several wilderness lakes, the court upheld the Forest Service's plan in full.

WHILE KEVIN PROESCHOLDT was awaiting word from the Forest Service, Clark Bullard, miles to the south in central Illinois, was readying his volunteer team for yet another round of protective work.

Bullard worked as an office-bound professor of mechanical engineering, but his heart was tied to a meandering, gravel-bottomed river some thirty miles east of his home. For years Bullard had defended this river, the Middle Fork of the Vermilion, against one attack after another. He was there, canoe paddle in hand, when nearby residents wanted to dam the river to attract industry. When the dam-building risk subsided, Bullard's loosely organized group, the Committee on the Middle Fork, began to push for legal protection for the stream. Their task was a difficult one, both because of local opposition and because the Middle Fork was not the kind of river that quickened the pulses and stirred the romantic yearnings of ordinary people. The Middle Fork contained no sparkling cataracts, no pounding white water, no towering ancient forests. It was simply a tree-lined prairie river, home to respectable populations of herons, kingfishers, minks, and horned owls; it was a river noteworthy mostly because it had survived years of human occupancy with fewer disturbances than other Illinois streams. Despite its lack of grandeur, Bullard and others loved the river. As a result of their efforts, in 1989 the Middle Fork of the Vermilion River became the only river in Illinois to be included in the National Wild and Scenic Rivers System.

A few years later, the principal industrial polluter on the river, the Illinois Power Company, asked the state's Pollution Control Board to relax the legal standards that protected the river's water quality. Illinois Power operated an old coal-burning electricity generating plant not far from the riverbank, and it wanted to continue polluting as it had done for decades, allowing overflow from its ash ponds to pour into the river. But to carry on business as usual, Illinois Power needed to circumvent the terms of its new, tougher discharge permit, soon to go into effect.

The company hired a team of lawyers from Chicago, who in turn found scientists to testify that the coal ash was ecologically insignificant. Armed with selected bits of evidence, Illinois Power argued that the ash did no harm and that utility ratepayers shouldn't pay higher rates for pollution-control measures that yielded no benefit.

Illinois Power's litigation war chest was well stocked; Bullard, by contrast, could scrape together only enough money for photocopying costs. The Illinois chapter of the Sierra Club agreed to support Bullard's group, but it, too, had little money. Like many environmental groups, the club's conservation programs were mostly run by volunteers.

Bullard's team nonetheless rose to the occasion, testifying at a hearing that lasted for several days and submitting a lengthy brief. Illinois Power's data, Bullard claimed, were too scanty and ambiguous to support the no-harm allegation. No one knew how the

Middle Fork had changed under the burden of forty years' exposure to Illinois Power's coal-ash effluent. In the absence of clear knowledge, Bullard argued, the more prudent policy was to err on the side of safety. Bullard also took strong issue with Illinois Power's exclusive focus on the modest effect of its pollution on the river's human users. He also wanted to know about the ash's effect on the fish that lived there and the wild animals that came to the river to drink. The water wasn't used to irrigate crops, but what of the aquatic plants growing in the stream and the animal life that depended on the plants? Who knew how the pollution's effects rippled through the biotic community?

In due course, the Illinois Pollution Control Board handed down its ruling, a unanimous decision in favor of Bullard's Committee on the Middle Fork. The board agreed that Illinois Power lacked evidence to justify its no-harm claim. It also agreed that pollution standards existed to protect the river itself and its biotic community, not just the river's current human users. Illinois Power, though, was undeterred by this legal setback and appealed to the Illinois courts. Frustrated by the delays and convinced that Illinois Power would drag its feet interminably, Bullard and his colleagues took the offensive. Claiming that Illinois Power was violating the federal Clean Water Act, the Committee on the Middle Fork announced it would file suit in federal court.

The suit was never filed. Later that fall, the Appellate Court of Illinois upheld the action of the Illinois Pollution Control Board, agreeing that the Illinois Power Company had failed to prove the absence of harm to the river. Soon thereafter, and largely for unrelated reasons, the utility mothballed its Middle Fork power plant, retaining it only for emergency use.

THE INDICTMENTS

Taken together, these three scenes illustrate the complexities of the ongoing debate about how people ought to live on the planet—

about what precisely it means to own land, about the ecological and spiritual values of wild places, and about how people should assess environmental risks and legislate pollution limits when their knowledge is incomplete. In these scenes and others, economic calculations play a role: Many land-use practices simply make no financial sense, even when long-term harms are discounted to present value. But for many people, the ultimate environmental issue is not primarily one of dollars and cents; it is more deep-seated than that, a mixture of ecology and ethics, a matter that relates fundamentally to a person's responsibilities to the surrounding social and ecological communities.

One recurring concern in environmental disputes is that people are now so divorced from the land that we've forgotten what we once knew intimately: that we depend, ultimately, on the land for our nourishment, shelter, health, and happiness. The ready assumption is that food comes from the grocery store; that wastes disappear once the garbage truck drives away; and that humans can somehow lead healthy lives while other species sicken and disappear. These assumptions simply aren't right, scientifically or ethically, and they very much need to change. The land is a complicated, organic whole, with people an integral part of that whole, as enmeshed in the natural order as the osprey and the otter. To accompany declarations of political independence, nations might usefully issue declarations of natural *inter*dependence as a means of recognizing and proclaiming these undeniable links.

The obvious interconnectedness of life has led many environmentalists to question the human-centeredness, or anthropocentrism, that underlies so much of modern thought. In the sixteenth century, French mathematician and philosopher René Descartes asserted that the pained cries of a tortured animal were the same as noise from a machine's grinding gears: Neither machines nor animals had minds or souls, which meant that neither counted for anything morally. This Renaissance wisdom strikes many today as arrogant and misguided. Why is it that humans matter in moral terms and other species do not? What makes people so special that human life alone is morally important? Rancher Clayton Williams denied that other animals have legitimate claims to their surrounding world when he sought to assert private ownership of the elk and antelopes on his high-plains fiefdom. So, too, did the Illinois Power Company when it argued that its continued pollution was acceptable because no people drank the water.

In the quest to revalue nonhuman forms of life, animal welfare advocates have taken the visible lead, urging that moral value, if not something akin to human rights, should extend to members of higher-functioning species. More ecologically oriented critics are prone to extend moral value not to individual animals but to organizing entities such as species, ecosystems, or entire biotic regions. In this view, the loons of the Boundary Waters Canoe Area have value as a species, aside from whatever value they might have as individual organisms and whatever aesthetic value people might assign to them. Similarly, the Middle Fork of the Vermilion River is a morally worthy biotic community regardless of the value of each component piece.

In a worldview in which humans alone count, the land becomes a mere tool or instrument that possesses value only insofar as it betters human existence. Right and wrong are determined by looking solely at how an action affects human pleasure or well-being, and the most moral approach to land use is the one that maximizes human good. Economic reasoning and cost-benefit analyses draw strength from this utilitarian way of viewing nature, and so does a great deal of ordinary public discourse. Protecting the snail darter makes sense, many people think, only if humans, on balance, will directly benefit from it.

Utilitarian thinking such as this has received considerable criticism from environmentalists. An obvious question they raise is why the interests of other species aren't taken into account, either as individual organisms or as collective entities. What of the wolves of Minnesota and the locally endangered bluebreast darter, resident of the Middle Fork of the Vermilion? They, too, have interests that a more full calculation could take into account, and so does the Wyoming mule deer herd. Then, too, there is the matter of future generations of humans, if not future generations of other species. They also have interests that a utility calculation should include. Even if people today aren't using the Middle Fork to irrigate crops, what if future generations need to do so?

Aside from these challenges posed by other species and future generations, there is the problem that arises from nature's sheer complexity. If the wise, morally correct choice in a given controversy is the one that achieves the most good, then it becomes essential to identify and weigh all the consequences that flow from alternative courses of action. Yet it's often impossible to perform such calculations in more than a rudimentary way, given nature's intense complexity and the limits of human knowledge. Indeed, even when the effects of a particular action can be traced, it's often hard to distinguish a harmful effect from a beneficial one without an ethically and ecologically informed measure of value. So great are these challenges, many people think, that utilitarian calculations alone simply cannot provide a good compass.

Consider a grassy Illinois meadow torn up by a plow and replaced with a field of corn. Economists can calculate the value of the corn, at least in market terms, but what about the other changes brought on by the plowing? Where meadowlarks and bobolinks once nested in the meadow, red-winged blackbirds and crows now reside. A change in bird populations has plainly occurred, but is the change beneficial or harmful, given the birds' differing behaviors? And how could one quantify that change in order to weigh it along with the many other resulting changes? Other factors, such as the soil loss caused by perennial plowing, are also awkward to measure and value, assuming they're noted at all. More complicated still are the effects that spill beyond the boundaries of the farm field. What happens when the eroded soil washes into the nearby stream, muddying its waters? Will the big-eye chubs in the stream die because they can no longer spot food in the dirty water? And will their demise in turn contribute to a shift in the river's overall aquatic life?

Cases like these highlight the obvious limits of human knowledge, and they've prompted many critics to raise pointed questions about the ways people acquire knowledge of nature and about the constraints imposed by limited human senses. To the modern mind, accurate knowledge about nature is obtained in only one way—through empirical data collected by human senses. In rigorous analyses, knowledge not based on observable data is cast aside or viewed with suspicion. Once the empirical facts are in, conclusions are drawn by the process of deductive reasoning. Whatever its virtues may be in controlled experimental settings, this reasoning method has no way to deal with the incompleteness of data, nor can it overcome the biases introduced by human assumptions and the limits of human perception. Thus, the many unknowns of nature, such as species never seen and ripple effects never traced, are often left out of data-bound environmental assessments.

The Illinois Power Company sought to capitalize on this tendency to ignore unknowns when it argued that its effluent didn't affect the Middle Fork. In reality, the company had tested its effluent on only one species of fish—a common minnow—and then only to see whether the fish would die within three days. The company knew even less about its effluent's effects on aquatic plants. In the face of its ignorance, Illinois Power assumed that no harm was occurring; even one dollar spent on cleanup, it claimed, would go to waste. The Committee on the Middle Fork urged a more cautious route. The cost of halting all water pollution, Bullard calculated, was less than five cents per customer per month. Given the degree of human ignorance, given the river's sensitivity and its unique value—surely this small expenditure for pollution control was money well spent.

As many environmental activists see it, the time has come for people to steer a different, less arrogant course, one that admits human ignorance and seeks to adjust for it. Before the modern age, people viewed nature as a mysterious, powerful force. They did their best to understand nature empirically, but they supplemented that knowledge with their intuitions and sentiments about nature. Often, their intuitions were ethical ones that recognized spirits and values in the world around them and prompted a more restrained, humble attitude toward the land.

People today need to resurrect some of these older ways of relating to the vast natural world. Decision-making processes need to become less data dependent; they need to incorporate humility with ignorance so that people act more gently toward the land and leave room to correct their inevitable mistakes. Humility is particularly needed when estimating the value of nature's parts and setting burdens of proof on environmental issues. Rather than assuming that a plant or an animal is worthless unless the contrary is clearly proven or that a new chemical or land-use practice is ecologically benign, the wise approach is to err on the side of caution, using a far lower burden of proof when concerns are raised about the land's long-term health.

To push for greater humility with respect to the land is not to discount the importance of science or its applied cousin, technology. When viewed as it should be—as a method of gaining knowledge—science is an indispensable tool. Without good science, far less would be known about environmental challenges and how to deal with them. And without good technology, pollution-control measures would work less well. The problem with science lies not with the scientific method but with the larger culture that has arisen around it. Society tends to presume that science has all the answers and that scientific knowledge can determine how people ought to live without any need for fundamental values or ethical choices. On a more dangerous level, some even think that science ultimately will liberate people from nature's limits. The drawback of technology is that it, too, can be bad as well as good, productive of disease as well as health, depending on the purposes it serves.

Far from opposing science, activists such as Clark Bullard call for even more of it, particularly for further basic research into nature's ways of functioning. More monitoring needs to be done of water, air, and plant and animal life. Indeed, one of the best ways to act humbly toward the land is to become more attentive to its details. The arrogant way—the path too often pursued—is to alter the land without taking time to study it or to slash funding for environmental research on the premise that a problem not recognized is a problem easily ignored. In many instances, environmental groups play the role of technology optimists: They are the ones pushing for cars that can average 100 miles per gallon, for renewable energy sources to replace fossil fuels, for an end to toxic wastes, and for holistic, healthier farming practices.

The environmental call for humility is part of a more fundamental criticism of human domination, a criticism that cuts at the very heart of the democratic, liberal understanding of the world. Ever since the Enlightenment, Western culture has exalted the individual human as the prime measure of value. Whether in philosophy or psychology, law or medicine, value rests discretely in each person. But this understanding conflicts with basic axioms of the natural world. No organism, human or otherwise, can live in isolation. All organisms interact constantly with their surroundings, gaining energy and nutrients, returning wastes, and bumping and pounding against other life-forms and inorganic matter. Clayton Williams encountered this axiom of interconnectedness when he sought to divide his range from the surrounding biotic community, as if hunting on his land had no spillover effects. The natural order, plainly, is far more than just a collection of independent parts. As farmer and writer Wendell Berry put it, "no matter how sophisticated and complex and powerful our institutions, we are still exactly as dependent on the earth as the earthworms."

This holistic, ecological attitude now dominates environmental thinking, and its potential disruptiveness to contemporary society is hard to overstate. The most prominent articulation of holism remains Aldo Leopold's land ethic, lyrically expressed in the concluding essay of *A Sand County Almanac:* "A thing is right when it tends to preserve the integrity, stability, and beauty of the biotic community. It is wrong when it tends otherwise." The community, not the individual member, has primary moral value in Leopold's ethic. Holistic thinking such as this offers a sharp challenge to the dominant political philosophies, from liberalism to libertarianism, that aim to enhance private happiness rather than any particular conception of the public good. A community-oriented land ethic inevitably shrinks and reconfigures an individual's sphere of personal liberty as practices long thought innocuous are seen to cause harm.

Any worldview that focuses on the individual level—on the parts—inevitably creates difficulties when used to describe humans in nature. We need ways of conceiving our place in the world that begin with our interconnectedness and that consider the individual person less as a discrete unit and more as a locus or node of forces and interactions. People can still be viewed as special, but as special parts of something larger, and dependent in the long term on the health and well-being of that larger whole.

NEW BEARINGS

Contemporary culture, in short, needs new bearings in the natural order. It needs a broader understanding of moral value and a better grasp of the limits of utilitarian calculations. Empiricism and reason need to yield space to sentiment, intuition, and humility, and the myths surrounding science's powers need chipping away even while scientists expand their knowledge. Most of all, what's needed is a more holistic view of the world, one in which humans no longer stand so conspicuously above and apart from other life-forms.

But if new bearings are to provide guidance for real-life controversies, they need to come together in a concrete, practical way.

They need to fit together into a long-term goal that is explicit enough to stand as a polestar or benchmark for resolving disputes about using land and other parts of nature. Criticisms are useful, but to provide guidance they need to be transformed into a positive statement of how humans ought to live, a statement that draws upon good science and sound ethics. In its early days, the environmental movement got by without such a goal; a sense of outrage over visible degradation provided guidance enough. But controversies have become more subtle and contentious. Moral outrage is a blunt tool, useful when evil actors are easily identified but less helpful when situations are complex and people are confused.

But what exactly would such a goal look like? What does it mean to live morally in a land already pushed hard by humanity? What processes are most likely to succeed in getting people to recognize their shared fate and inspiring them to work to improve it? And ultimately, what does it really mean for a natural community to be healthy?

Chapter 3

Setting a Course

W HEN THE SNAIL darter case arrived on the public scene
in the mid-1970s, environmentalism was more a virtuous impulse than an orderly call for a new orientation toward nature. Its voice was loud, but its direction was unclear. In
contrast, the contemporaneous civil rights movement possessed a
simple, understandable goal: freedom and equality for all individuals. So, too, did the market-oriented strand of conservative
thought: efficient allocation of resources for maximum social
wealth. Both of these causes gained strength by having goals that
were so easily grasped. Compared with them, the environmental
movement was diffuse and confused. It, too, had something to do
with individual freedom, the freedom to breathe clean air and
enjoy nature's beauty, but it limited other freedoms by denying individuals the right to despoil community resources. Environmentalism also had something to do with the efficient use of natural re-

sources, but its view of efficiency was far different from and more complex than that of the conservative right.

Even today, environmentalism lacks a single, simple goal. And it needs one, a goal that makes sense and is inspiring, if it is to gain ground in the new century. The task of setting an environmental goal, however, is not an easy one. Efforts to articulate one began back in the heyday of environmental lawmaking, in the 1960s and early 1970s. The United States Congress at the time was paying close attention to environmental problems, and in rapid-fire fashion it dispatched a wide array of statutes, from laws protecting marine mammals and coastal zones to laws limiting drilling on federal lands and mandating the restoration of old mining sites. As it drafted laws, Congress inevitably needed to explain their purposes. What problems were the laws intended to solve? What were the statutes intended to accomplish?

Between the late 1960s and the late 1970s, Congress took various stabs at identifying the causes of environmental ills and setting goals. Looking back, one is struck by the naiveté of the time, particularly the early years. Faith in congressional power was high, far too high. In addition, too few people really understood that seemingly distinct problems—air pollution, water pollution, endangered species—were all interconnected. Environmental ills weren't the superficial difficulties many people supposed, easily wiped away while everyday life plugged along. They arose from the industrial market economy and the day-to-day living practices of ordinary people. They stemmed from prevailing ways of dividing and valuing the land, from ecological ignorance, and from immature moral thought. And they reflected a deeply competitive individualism that weakened the sense of community. These were serious challenges, ones that a few laws wouldn't soon overcome.

In time, Congress began offering more sober descriptions of problems and setting more modest legislative aims. Congress soon recognized that it could deal with big corporations that spewed pollution but it was less able to alter the day-to-day practices of ordinary citizens. Some problems were simply too local and too close to the land to remedy from Washington.

The record of Congress's work, its successes and its failures, provides useful lessons for the new century. It shows the sheer difficulty of identifying a clear long-term goal, given nature's complexity. It shows, too, the important ethical issues that are woven in with the pragmatic and scientific issues, making the course-charting task all the more difficult. Finally, it displays the limits of the ability of any single level of government, even one as powerful as the federal government of the United States, to deal with the full range of environmental problems, from issues of global policy to individual life choices.

The Congressional Record

Congress began its main burst of environmental lawmaking with the National Environmental Policy Act of 1969. NEPA remains in force and little changed today, reflective of the thoughts and aspirations that prevailed when it was written. In its introductory sections, NEPA speaks of "restoring and maintaining environmental quality," of "creat[ing] and maintain[ing] conditions under which man and nature can exist in productive harmony," and of "the responsibilities of each generation as trustee of the environment for succeeding generations." At the time of their writing, these goals sounded impressive and were seriously meant, but one wonders what the lawmakers had in mind. What was meant by environmental "quality," and how did one go about measuring it? What did it mean for humans to interact with nature in "productive harmony"? If people were trustees for the future, what were their duties, and where could they find a copy of the trust agreement? Neither NEPA nor its legislative history offered any answers.

Aside from its ambiguous language, NEPA was simplistic in its attempt to accomplish these goals merely by requiring the preparation of environmental impact assessments before major federal projects were undertaken. Indeed, in drafting NEPA, lawmakers seemed to view the nation's ecological plight not as a problem of crabbed values or narrow moral vision but as one merely of incomplete information. With the right information, agency heads could make healthy choices; handed the right data, they would further the goal of ecological harmony Congress had so loftily proclaimed.

The information-based approach exemplified by NEPA was not new in 1969. Nearly a decade earlier, in the Multiple-Use Sustained-Yield Act of 1960, Congress had sought to improve forest-management decisions by pressing officials to consider multiple uses of forests, including recreation and wildlife, before setting loose the tree-cutting crews. By the terms of the act, the Forest Service was expected to pick "the combination that [would] best meet the needs of the American people," which was "not necessarily the combination of uses that [would] give the greatest dollar return or the greatest unit output." And the Forest Service was to do this, Congress pronounced, "without impairment of the productivity of the land."

Despite its promising language, the Multiple-Use Sustained-Yield Act did little to reshape agency values and practices. Litigants cited it when challenging timber clear-cutting and other tree-farming practices, but courts deemed the statute too vague to enforce. After all, how could the courts determine—how could anyone determine—what combination of land uses would "best meet the needs of the American people"? In practice, the act slowed clear-cutting only a bit; the values and politics of timber were simply too entrenched, within government and without, for misty oratory to uproot them. At most, the statute softened old ways of thinking by adding a quiet note of restraint: By interjecting the notion of sustainability into the law, it raised the prospect that future generations might soon count for more than they had.

Both NEPA and the Multiple-Use Sustained-Yield Act directed federal agencies to take better care of the environment, leaving the agencies free to select whatever protective measures seemed most appropriate. But flexibility inevitably meant discretion, and discretion inevitably meant that agencies were free to charge ahead as they always had, largely ignoring environmental values in the rush to cut trees, build freeways, and dam rivers. NEPA called for greater stewardship but didn't mandate it. Although meant to promote the land's health, it neither defined its goal clearly nor explained the human role in it. In practice, NEPA achieved many good results, mostly by getting the public more involved in resource-use decisions, but its accomplishments fell far short of its aims.

During the early 1970s, as Congress addressed various pollution and hazardous-waste problems, it continued to take hesitant steps toward a more holistic view of the land. In its statute restricting ocean dumping, for instance, it expressed concerns not only about dumping "which would adversely affect human health, welfare, or amenities" but also about "the marine environment" and its "ecological systems." Similarly, when Congress tightened the toxic emissions provisions of the Clean Air Act, it spoke of threats to the health of soils, wildlife, and other elements of ecosystems as well as threats to human health. Perhaps most prominently, the Federal Water Pollution Control Act of 1972, commonly referred to as the Clean Water Act, aimed to "restore and maintain the chemical, physical, and biological integrity of the Nation's waters."

Unfortunately, these advanced statutory pronouncements appeared only in precatory, introductory language, not in substantive legal provisions that would actually restrict what polluters could do. As the Middle Fork controversy illustrates, actual pollution policies dwell far more on near-term adverse effects on people than on the integrity and functioning of ecosystems. Water-quality standards, for instance, are based on human uses of each waterway, with pollution considered "acceptable" so long as it doesn't undercut those uses and with the unknown effects of pollution largely ignored. Under the Clean Water Act as implemented, waterway integrity simply has not counted for much.

Over the years, Congress has shown the greatest ecological sensitivity in its statutes dealing with wild resources. Yet even in these laws, intellectual and moral limits are evident. In the Wilderness Act of 1964, Congress waxed grandly about the values of wilderness to "present and future generations" of people, enumerating many values that were distinctly nonutilitarian. Yet the processes Congress prescribed for selecting wilderness preserves, then and in later statutes, largely ignored surrounding ecosystems. Wilderness areas were viewed as isolated enclaves, chosen on the basis of political considerations and availability. Preservation was a matter of putting particular lands to best use, not a matter of using publicly owned lands in ways that promoted the well-being of entire regions.

By the 1990s, Congress had designated 100 million acres of wilderness, yet it had no real vision of how wilderness preservation might fit into a larger environmental policy or plan. Wilderness preservation became a hodgepodge process, with some lands set aside while others were freed for intensive development. The message conveyed, sometimes overtly, was that preservation of particular lands justified degradation of other lands. In an almost tit-for-tat mentality, wilderness areas, it seemed, could exist—and would have to exist—as pockets of little-touched nature in a deteriorating landscape, with their boundaries alone protecting them.

A second message implicit in the preservation process was that people inevitably defiled the land and the only effective way to preserve a tract was to set it off limits. To many observers, this message sounded misanthropic, and the charge of misanthropy was quickly leveled at pro-preservation groups. Roadless areas became battlegrounds between those who wanted development and those who sought to "lock up" lands so people couldn't benefit from them. As long as wilderness areas were perceived as enclaves, preservation did seem to mean locking places up, with environmentalists apparently concerned more about grizzly bears than about people. More enlightened legislation might have justified such enclaves by noting how nature preserves foster the health of surrounding areas and thus benefit the people living there. But Congress couldn't legislate in this way without itself taking an unprecedented step in the direction of ecosystem-oriented thinking.

The Endangered Species Act of 1973 represented Congress's most prominent step toward such holistic thinking. The act's first-listed goal wasn't to preserve imperiled species; it was to conserve "the ecosystems upon which endangered species and threatened species depend. . . ." The act directed the U.S. Fish and Wildlife Service to promote this ecological aim by protecting the critical habitat of imperiled species and by formulating plans for their recovery. The act also banned the killing or "taking" of endangered animals, which included the material destruction of their critical habitat.

Despite these provisions, the Endangered Species Act has proved less revolutionary than its language suggests. In practice, the act operates much as does the Wilderness Act—preserving wild spots beyond the reach of human activity but doing little to challenge the degradation of human-occupied places. The U.S. Fish and Wildlife Service typically doesn't protect all the habitat needed for a listed species to flourish. Instead, it protects only those lands minimally needed to avoid near-term extinction, and even then only when the economic costs aren't too high. It rarely prosecutes landowners who destroy important habitat areas, and it freely issues "incidental take" permits sanctioning land-use practices that impair prospects for species recovery.

The difficulty Congress ran into when protecting species was the same difficulty it encountered when protecting wilderness areas and pursuing other environmental aims. Too many environmental problems were tied, directly or indirectly, to private land, and Congress couldn't deal with them effectively without tinkering with landowner rights. Water pollution couldn't be controlled without limits on runoff pollution from fields, managed forests, and other private lands. And most endangered species lived partially or even wholly on private lands. Congress, though, had never played a role in the regulation of land use. Landed property rights had arisen under state law, and state and local governments controlled them.

Private property ownership has been an exalted idea in American culture since the first settlers at Jamestown pressed the Virginia Company to grant them individual tracts of land. Until the modern age, property law primarily addressed social and political concerns, not ecological ones. In essence, property law gave a landowner the right to ward off meddlesome neighbors and to resist an overreaching state. It also protected economic investments, allowing landowners to sow in the spring with the comfortable expectation that the fall crop would be theirs to harvest. What property law didn't do was reflect concern about the land's degradation and the well-being of other species. Indeed, an owner had broad powers to destroy or consume the land as he or she saw fit. And when land was damaged by an outsider, the legal injury was to the human owner, not to the land itself.

In urban settings, landowner autonomy has diminished under an outpouring of zoning ordinances and health and safety rules. But in rural areas, old ideas of landownership remain strong. Clayton Williams may have lost his suit against Wyoming, but his vision lives on. During its flurry of environmental lawmaking in the 1970s, Congress considered several options for altering landowner rights to serve environmental goals. But the idea of federal interference in individual property rights quickly met with strong resistance, so strong that Congress backed away. Proposals for federal land-use planning quickly died, as did meaningful proposals to protect farmland, to regulate private forestry activities, and to control land uses as a means of containing diffuse sources of water pollution.

In retrospect, Congress probably did as much as it reasonably could to deal with environmental problems comprehensively.

Although members of Congress understood the essentials of ecology and were prepared to value wilderness areas and rare species, they lacked a clear sense of how people ought to live on the land in healthy, sustainable ways. Environmental policy inevitably rests on moral values, and Congress was reluctant to wander too far into controversial moral terrain. Congress was further hampered by its mandate to address only nationwide issues. It could deal with pollution emitted by industries competing in national and international markets and with conservation of federally owned resources. But it had no jurisdiction over activities with little or no connection to the national economy, and it viewed nonfederal land uses as the responsibility of other levels of government, those closer to the people.

Given these limits, Congress inevitably approached environmental problems piecemeal, leaving to others the work of integrating pieces into landscape-scale plans. Wilderness areas were preserved but were not joined with surrounding lands. Rare species were preserved as national assets, but the full biological diversity of particular landscapes was not. Similarly, river navigation and flooding were national concerns, but they couldn't be addressed fully without tampering with ordinary drainage practices and land-use issues in towns and on farms everywhere. Federal laws alone couldn't solve major problems; other levels of government had to get involved, down to the smallest drainage district and township road board, and greater citizen participation was needed as well.

Congress, then, was hamstrung because critical pieces were beyond its control, pieces so important that no coherent policy could be assembled without them. Unfortunately, Congress was slow to realize its limits, and in the early years it attacked problems alone, responding to one headline-news challenge after another. States were penciled in to help implement the Clean Air Act and the Clean Water Act, but policy guidance flowed only from the top. States had trivial roles in the management of wilderness areas, parks, and national forests; if they chose to coordinate their own efforts with federal plans, they did so on their own initiative. In addition, federal endangered species programs were poorly coordinated with state wildlife efforts and rarely addressed matters of ecosystem integrity.

As Congress charged ahead, state and local governments lagged in their remedial efforts, although they, too, had successes. These governments, to be sure, also faced limits on what they could do. Economic and political constraints hemmed them in, and they were powerless to deal with such problems as interstate pollution. Moreover, many state and local governments ran the risk of losing workers to other places if their laws became too onerous. Still, these lower levels of government had vital roles to play and broad powers to deploy. Many of them had experience in regulating mining, timber cutting, and other resource activities. Urban governments in particular were comfortable in setting limits on what private landowners could do. Just as important, many local governments could draw citizens into governing processes, creating effective channels of communication and promoting behavior changes in less peremptory and threatening ways.

The Goal of Land Health

Clearly, no single level of government can combat the entire environmental challenge alone. Even when governments possess power, they're often reluctant to tackle matters with strong ethical overtones absent a clear consensus among citizens. For an overall environmental goal to come together, one that incorporates all the pieces, action by people outside government must come first—by organizations and citizens better able to step back and take stock of the entire landscape, embracing people, who are bounded in their traditions and capabilities, and imagining ways for them to live in a naturally boundless land.

An overall environmental goal needs to arise from the bedrock reality of ecological interconnectedness, and it needs to focus not directly on human well-being but on the well-being of the overall land community, broadly understood to include the soil, water, and air, as well as resident humans, other animals, and plants. A land community *can* be more or less healthy, in terms of the elements and processes essential to bountiful life, even while its resident species and other pieces change over time. And that health needs to become the central preoccupation and goal of environmental policy. Better than any alternative, land health can serve as the clear expression of purpose that environmentalism very much needs. Efforts to deal with specific environmental problems should aim to promote this goal, and it needs to become a core value of modern culture.

But what exactly is land health? When Aldo Leopold spoke of land health in *A Sand County Almanac,* he focused on the land's basic needs: conserving soil, maintaining water flows and water quality, and mitigating significant human-caused changes in species populations. Since Leopold expressed these views in the 1940s, scientists have become better skilled at identifying the conditions that contribute to the land's vigor and resilience. Much is now known, for instance, about the efficiency of plants in capturing solar energy and converting it to forms of energy that other organisms can use. There are studies, too, of the role of wetlands in filtering water flows so that organisms dependent on clean water can survive, and there are population studies showing that some species are more critical to ecosystem functioning than others. Overall, land health can be defined scientifically as nature's ability to keep doing what it has long done—building and retaining soil, clothing the land with lush vegetation, cleansing water flows, capturing sunlight and moving energy through multiple trophic levels, pulling minerals from the subsoil and cycling them through predation chains, and, ultimately, giving rise to new life-forms able to find or create suitable niches.

A useful, if limited, analogy can be drawn between land health and an individual organism's health. Much as an organism's long-term health depends on sensible living in a clean environment, not just on the treatment of disease, land health requires more than plugging pollution pipes and restraining overconsumption. The comparison, though, should not be pushed too far. A land community doesn't operate as an individual organism does; it is more variable in composition and less amenable to application of simple, quick remedies, akin to the antibiotic that rids an organism of disease. In addition, a land community has less distinct boundaries and thus presents a greater restoration challenge. Finally, the health of an organism is more objectively assessed, with fewer ethical complexities. Still, land health is a meaningful and inspiring idea, and as scientific knowledge of the land accumulates, it becomes more measurable as well.

At the same time, the idea of land health is distinguishable from the popular, vaguely phrased idea of sustainable development, which the United Nations and other bodies have embraced. Sustainable development is a valuable concept insofar as it draws attention to the need for people to live in ways that can be repeated for generations without degrading the land. Yet sustainable development also has severe drawbacks, at least as the term is commonly understood.

To begin with, wide disagreement exists on the meaning of sustainable development. To some, the term *sustainable* implies the continuation of particular types of economic activities or human lifestyles, without direct reference to the proper functioning of natural ecosystems. But it makes no sense to talk about sustaining a timber economy that is based on the cutting of old-growth forests or sustaining farm practices that destroy soil and pollute water. The term *development*, though also not well defined, generally refers to economic processes that are simply not sustainable. As commonly understood, development consumes ever greater parts of nature and pushes ecological processes and systems closer and closer to collapse: It pulls against the idea of sustainability, leaving the sum of the words in doubt.

Sustainable development also fails to capture the ethical complexity of human interactions with the rest of nature. *Development* suggests a process in which people are in charge, manipulating the land to their increasing advantage. The term carries no connotation of humility and implies no limit to the manipulative process. The success of development is measured by human-constructed scales, not by measures put in place by nature. Development generates good things for present-day humans, not for the natural community or for future human generations.

The goal of land health, in contrast, looks far beyond the well-being of humans: Other species live on the land, and if the land as a whole is valuable, they, too, are valuable. Health, moreover, is both a natural matter and a mysterious process, something understood through collection of empirical data but also grasped in part through intuition, sentiment, and other ways of making sense of the unknown. In short, land health encompasses the kind of durable, flourishing, self-recreating communal life that is the mark of a lasting link between people and place.

The Ethics of Land Health

To think of the land solely in scientific terms is to ignore many potent ethical claims, ones that have engaged people for centuries and become particularly intense over the past century. For Albert Schweitzer a century ago, the ethical landscape was easily described: All life was sanctified and deserved his great respect. For most observers, however, nature is more varied in its moral features, requiring greater discernment and continuing moral clarification. As an overall goal, the concept of land health needs to incorporate these moral considerations, whether simple or complex. That is, it needs to extend beyond mere scientific depiction of a vigorous land to describe a land that flourishes in response to ethically mature human behavior.

From the perspective of land health, ethical questions arise not only about nature's inherent value but also about the ways various people get to use nature. Access to food and the land's economic opportunities raises obvious ethical issues. Questions also arise about opportunities people have to enjoy nature and to participate in its processes—opportunities, for instance, to see rare plants and animals, to experience various types of wilderness, and to relish the solace and sense of escape that can be experienced in open spaces. People may conclude that they and their descendants have the right to experience nature little touched by human hands. These ethical considerations also need to figure into land health.

For some environmentalists, the ethical component of environmental thought is essentially religious in orientation, dealing as it does with the rightful place of humans in the order of creation. On this point, Protestant Christians have been most prominent. Some have turned to nature for insights about how people ought to live, viewing nature as a divine creation embedded with spiritual and ethical lessons; others have looked to time-honored scriptures for guidance. Although religious traditions differ, a common ending point is that the land and everything on it is divinely created or infused with God's presence or spirit. As such, it is worthy of awe and respect.

Ethical thought also pays considerable attention to future generations. As many environmentalists see things, people now living have a duty to leave the land healthy, biologically rich, and aesthetically pleasing for future generations. For some, this duty provides the core ethical reason for taking care of the land. Other observers, equally concerned about the long term, find it awkward to talk of future generations in terms of rights and duties. More sensible, they claim, is to speak of the virtue of restraint. They sense a wisdom in leaving options open for future generations, without need for resorting to a refined theory of moral rights.

A related question has to do with the moral worth of other lifeforms, as individual organisms, as species, and collectively as natural communities. Many species plainly have practical value to humans: Some are directly valuable because they provide food, fiber, and medicines; others are indirectly valuable because of their roles in supporting and sustaining ecological communities. Species preservation, some people argue, is simply prudent, for humans may never know the value of a species until the day comes when it is needed. Aldo Leopold presented the point this way:

> *If the land mechanism as a whole is good, then every part is good, whether we understand it or not. If the biota, in the course of aeons, has built something we like but do not understand, then who but a fool would discard seemingly useless parts? To keep every cog and wheel is the first precaution of intelligent tinkering.*

For some environmentalists, the value of other species extends beyond the practical: All species have an inherent right to exist, regardless of any benefit they provide for humans.

Although environmental thought reflects disagreement about the best way to value species, most advocates believe that individual plants and animals are less important than species and the land community as a whole. Perspectives that focus on the rights or welfare of individual animals pay too little attention to community well-being. In the common environmental view, hunting, fishing, and trapping can help maintain the land community, particularly when used to control species whose populations have expanded excessively as a result of human activities.

The upshot of this varied ethical literature is this: Human uses of the land raise ethical issues as well as pragmatic ones. Accordingly, as an overall goal, land health needs to include an ethical element as well as a pragmatic one. A healthy land is a land that flourishes in response to ethical human behavior as well as functioning productively in ways scientists can study.

When Aldo Leopold wrote about land health, his remarks often touched on ethical issues. For him, land health reached beyond the best empirical science to include his seasoned intuitions and his long-simmering ethical values. As Leopold knew, a healthy land is a place vibrant and productive in ecological terms, but it is, importantly, more and other than that. Healthy lands are lands people deal with in ways that are ethically responsible. If ethical treatment means behaving with due respect for the options of future generations, then a healthy land is one that preserves those options. If ethical treatment includes respect for all species of plants and animals, then a healthy land is one on which other species are sustained and protected, at least against human-induced extinction. If ethical treatment means the preservation of ecosystem types—because they are intrinsically worthy, because people should have chances to visit them, because they are divinely created, or for any other ethical reason—then a healthy land is one where ecosystem types are actively sustained, even aside from their utilitarian roles.

The ethical side of land health, plainly, is a messy one, requiring a good deal of reflection and a good many deliberate choices by people acting collectively. Yet it is a mistake to characterize such choices as mere matters of preference, with one view as good as the next. Ethical reasoning can also be objective in that its implementation requires good science and careful study. If species preservation is a moral imperative, as many people think it is, then conservation biologists must prepare preservation plans to help people live ethically. If a virtuous life includes an obligation to mitigate one's adverse effects on the land—as, again, many people think it does—then careful study is needed to identify those effects, particularly the distant, invisible ones, and to find ways to reduce them. As applied, then, the ethical side of land health mixes subjective and objective elements, just as the scientific side does.

The Challenges of Unruly Nature

Land health would be easier to achieve and, indeed, more readily recognized as primary if its scientific side were more clear. Ideally, ecologists could serve as expert witnesses and explain what it means for a land community to be healthy in a pragmatic sense. Ecology, though, has no such simple answers.

Modern ecologists, in fact, often cast doubt on the entire idea that identifiable natural communities exist. As many scientists describe it, an ecosystem is little more than a fluctuating collection of competing organisms, some succeeding better than others. Over time, communities naturally evolve, and as they change, entire species and groups of species come and go. Communities are disturbed by fire, storms, disease, pests, and invasions of nonnative species. These are natural occurrences, part of nature's way of doing business, and when they're taken into account, communities appear less stable and predictable. A forest recently cleared by fire, for instance, experiences rapid change in the plants that grow there as the pattern of vegetative succession unfolds. Such a forest is no less "natural" than a mature forest experiencing little observable change.

As particular communities evolve, they not only affect the species that compose them but also are themselves influenced by their constituent species, sometimes dramatically so. Elephants and gorillas materially alter the natural places where they live; they don't merely fit into open niches, leaving everything around them unchanged. This reality raises an inevitable and seemingly awkward question: If other species alter their environments, isn't it equally natural for humans to alter theirs? If elephants and gorillas can affect the mix of plants and animals around them, can't humans do the same?

Setting aside ethical issues, the difference is one of scale. Although natural communities do evolve over time, change often occurs slowly, in time frames much longer than human generations. Moreover, humans occupy nearly all parts of the globe, so the human geographic influence is vast. Then there is the magnitude of the change in many places. Humans have far more potent ways to reshape and contaminate the land than do other animals, and the human population is sufficiently large that even modest human practices can burden the land greatly. The estimated current rate of species loss highlights the difference. Species loss is a natural phenomenon, but the present rate of extinction is perhaps a thousand times greater than the background rate.

Although change, then, is natural, nature's communities are far more than just a collection of parts, randomly bouncing about. They fit together more snugly than this, constituting an interdependent whole with definable characteristics, even if that whole lacks enduring stability. As a community's biological and physical elements fit together, they give rise to ever greater levels of biological complexity and to emergent properties not present at the lower levels of organization. Hydrogen and oxygen, to use a simple example, come together as water, which has properties not present in the two elements separately. Bees in a hive show a social order and social functioning that are not present among solitary bees; the sum, again, is more than and different from its parts. Prairie plants fix nitrogen and produce carbohydrates better when acting together than any plant does when acting alone. The examples, truly, are endless.

Further evidence of community structure comes from the abundant work done on species that play specialty roles within a community and that depend for their existence on the continuation of part, much, or all of that structure. At work trying to unravel these complexities of biological communities are conservation and population biologists, whose studies reveal complex dependencies as well as ongoing change. Many species, it turns out, depend for their survival not only on particular other species and physical processes but also on the complexities and emergent properties created by and within the community structure. For such species, community structure is indispensably real.

Most recently, restoration ecologists, who struggle to reconstruct damaged ecosystems, have entered the arena of community-centered research. Their sobering experiences have shown how complex natural communities really are and how human efforts to create or reconstruct a natural community can quickly fail when community-level processes are poorly understood and imperfectly mimicked. A thriving natural community has the capacity to resist and recover from stress, including the full range of natural disturbances. It uses energy and nutrients with a high degree of efficiency, and it typically loses its efficiency, sometimes dramatically so, when materially disturbed. A healthy community also has the capacity for self-renewal; it is, in important ways, self-organizing and self-creating.

One explanation for the current emphasis within the field of ecology on nature's dynamism and flexibility may have to do with the present influence of population biologists and other scientists trained to look at nature from the bottom up, beginning with individual species and focusing on a community's evolving species composition. As often as not, scientists with this perspective find more chaos and change in nature than do scientists trained to look from the ecosystem level down, at energy and nutrient flows, at soil and biomass retention, and at hydrologic flows. A community can often retain its structure and internal functioning, even with broad, gradual shifts in its constituent species. To the outside observer, recent trends in ecology suggest a type of dialectical interaction between top-down and bottom-up approaches to the study of the land community; between talking about the coherence of communities as structured, functioning wholes and focusing instead on the sometimes radical incoherence of their constituent members over the long term. Academic fields, however, often progress by precisely this type of indirection, with new ideas overemphasized as a corrective to old ideas that were not quite right. Over the long term, both top-down and bottom-up approaches will probably remain quite useful in the continuing effort to make sense of nature's obscure ways. And as that work continues, the goal of land health will probably become more sound.

The "Is" and the "Ought"

When, late in life, Aldo Leopold pieced together his land ethic, he was well aware that communities fluctuated in composition. Indeed, he made a point of explaining to readers why the popular phrase *balance of nature* was inapt. He summed up his ethic by urging readers to preserve the "integrity, stability, and beauty" of ecological communities, yet in doing so he didn't presume a static community model.

Leopold was also well aware of how little scientists knew about nature. To him, a cautious, humble attitude only made sense. The wise approach, as he saw it, was to presume that even modest members of a land community had value and performed useful roles; they weren't simply excess parts that one could brush aside without thought. In *A Sand County Almanac*, Leopold made this point poignantly in a brief, lyrical essay on *Draba*, an early spring bloomer and "the smallest flower that blows." *Draba* is an unobtrusive flower, Leopold reported factually, one that botany books never picture and hikers rarely see. "No poets sing of it," he admitted. "Altogether it is of no importance—just a small creature that does a small job quickly and well."

Draba, Leopold wrote, merits honor not by being an indispensable keystone species, a plant that keeps an entire community together. Its job is more modest, and yet it is important nonetheless. Leopold liked it because of its beauty, because it blooms so early and so simply, and because it grows in sandy, shady places unattractive to more impressive plants. It is the botanical equivalent of everyman, one of nature's obscure ones. Other plants might perform its ecological work just as well. But *Draba* does the work that some plant has to do, and through evolution it has come to excel in its small niche. And for that, Leopold rejoiced.

Over time, the land ethic that Leopold crafted would inspire millions. Russian wildlife biologists would quote him; pirated editions of the *Almanac* would appear in China. Leopold would have liked this reception, for he wanted readers to see the land as he saw it and to value it as he did. His desire was not for government to impose his ethic on an unwilling people. Instead, he pinned his hopes on the minds and hearts of individual landowners and of citizens everywhere. He encouraged readers not merely to accept his teachings but to go beyond them. Implicitly, he urged that they, too, become spiritual pilgrims and grapple with the essential ethical dimensions of the link between humans and the land.

With hopes such as these, Leopold plainly wasn't proposing simply that readers let nature tell them how to live. Nature's ways—the "is" of nature—don't translate so directly or easily into the "ought" of human ethical norms. The process is more complex, and this would be so even if nature's ways were less obscure. What Leopold so fervently hoped was that as readers made their own land-use choices, their choices would reflect the kind of ethical humility he embraced.

Leopold proposed his land ethic as something a person could embrace individually, in one form or another. Land health, in contrast, is a collective goal, achievable only through the actions of many people. For land health to come about, even ethical landowners need to coordinate their work to deal with landscape-scale challenges. Collective work, however, fits uneasily into the contemporary mind. Robert Frost's fictional farmers carried on a tradition of cooperation, but it was modest in scope, a tradition that encouraged each to take care of his own. The achievement of land health will require more than this.

Perhaps no obstacles to the cooperative promotion of land health loom larger than the tradition of liberal individualism and the institution of the free-market economy. In tandem, these forces make it difficult for people to grasp a goal such as land health, much less to work together to achieve it. The key to dealing with these obstacles is first to understand them. And the way to understand them is to see how they operate in real life, to see how they influence the ways in which people view the land, value it, and put it to use.

Chapter 4

Grappling
with Individualism

THROUGH THE central parts of Champaign-Urbana, Illinois,
runs a narrow, winding creek that drains much of the community. Near the creek, the University of Illinois opened its
doors in 1867, and campus engineering buildings now crowd its
banks. On most days, the creek is unobtrusive, knowing its assigned
course and staying there. But after heavy rains, it sheds its tame
image and takes on a more menacing look, launching out of its
confining sides and roaming the neighborhoods nearby. To local
residents, the creek and its repeated flooding seem entirely natural, but as is often true, the seemingly natural has a distinct human
element to it. What local people have done to this creek and its
watershed, and the problems that persist here, offer useful insights

about land health—why it is an awkward concept for Americans to grasp and why its achievement will not come easily.

When the first settlers arrived in the area, in the 1830s, this prairie creek didn't exist in its current form. Then, the landscape was flush with a type of wetland known as a wet meadow, the product of a humid climate, flat lands, and slow natural drainage. Newly arriving farmers, not wanting fields that stayed wet too long in the spring, set about making changes. They devised ways to speed up the drainage, largely through networks of ditches and underground tiles. Later, scientists at the University of Illinois helped by developing drainage technology and testing new methods and equipment on land near the creek. As the use and the pace of drainage accelerated in the region, streams that were once lazy and meandering became more forceful. Water drained into the streams more quickly after each rainfall, and they became wider, deeper, and longer. They gained names and bridges and, at times, became much greater obstacles.

The human imprint on this neighborhood creek shows up in another way. When the first business owners set up shop many decades ago, they decided the creek was inconveniently located. Town planners envisioned a major street right where the creek was prone to meander. Acting on the shared attitudes of the era, local leaders did what only seemed appropriate: They moved the creek. The move was a short one, only a hundred yards or so, but the waters soon flowed along a new channel in a location different from what nature had in mind. When the rains come today, the creek seems to remember its old home, as if moved by ancestral instinct. Liberated by rising waters, the creek heads directly into what is now a crowded business district, to the consternation of business owners and the delight of sporting youths.

In appearance, this modest creek looks a good deal like urban creeks around the country, so much so that it needs little description. Once a winding, slow-moving stream lined with maples and cottonwoods and sycamores, it is now a tethered ditch, angular and rough. Broken concrete coats its banks, dumped there by the truckload to mitigate the erosive effects of unnaturally fast flows. Throughout the creek's length, its banks are adorned with trash, poked with drainage lines, and inhabited by rats. Along one of the better sections, a hopeful entrepreneur has turned an old lumber barn into a restaurant named Silver Creek. So far, though, the name has not caught on: Among locals, the waterway retains its former and more apt name, the Boneyard.

If one were to begin at Boneyard Creek near the center of town and wander north up its shallow watershed, the path would soon enter one of the poorest, most dilapidated neighborhoods of Champaign. A century ago, this area was economically vibrant, close to railroad terminals and desirable for residences and businesses alike. Today, the scene is less pleasing—homes in ill repair, abandoned vehicles and structures, and everywhere, in almost every block, empty lot after empty lot, dozens of them.

Along with its empty lots, this neighborhood north of the Boneyard has a considerable stock of underused people, people who have no work and no valued place in society. Some of these people are visible on the streets day by day; others, it seems, fade into the woodwork and shrubbery, living as invisibly as town leaders probably prefer them to do. Drugs are a problem here, and so is crime. Although this neighborhood has its uniqueness and its virtues, it typifies poor neighborhoods elsewhere, much as the Boneyard typifies abused urban creeks.

There is a great deal of ill health in this place, and it shows up in many ways. The creek itself is plainly sick, its waters polluted, its flow greatly distorted, and its wildlife largely limited to the rats and other opportunistic omnivores associated with dirty, human-occupied places everywhere. As a result, the creek is ugly, a community asset transformed through abuse into a community disgrace. Within the human community around the Boneyard, the visible forms of sickness are those that stem chiefly from inactivity and from the deterioration of social and economic structures.

Other forms of human sickness—evident in the detachment of people from the land, mentally and physically—are hidden from view. The creek itself is ignored, and the vacant lots stand idle. The land community, in short, has become dysfunctional.

The problems in this place have multiple origins. Yet they are framed and brought together by two dominant elements of contemporary culture—political and social individualism and the free-market economy. So strong are these cultural elements that they supply the lens through which the creek, the people, and the land are all understood and given context. But like other lenses, this lens distorts, and it does so in ways that continue to damage the health of the land community. Until these cultural elements are well understood and strategies are devised to mitigate their influence, a new land ethic will be slow to unfold.

The Weight of Individualism

Historian Louis Hartz observed decades ago that the story of America has been preeminently a story of ascending liberalism. By liberalism, Hartz meant not a particular political slant but a social and moral view that promoted the individual person and sought to liberate the individual from restraint. By focusing on the individual, liberalism departed from older European views of society, which wove people more tightly into social and economic systems and spoke of them in collective, status-bound terms, as members of tribes or villages or feudal orders. American liberalism first cropped up chiefly in the economic realm; the individual gained liberty largely in order to engage in more vigorous, unrestrained economic activities. From the economic realm, liberalism spread to political rights, to religion, and to social morality, leading ultimately to the predominantly atomistic social view of the present day. In each realm, liberalism gained ground by reducing constraints on individual choices and actions.

In its right-wing form, liberalism exalts pure liberty, often employing the rhetoric of libertarianism and free-market economics. The principal fear on the right is the infringement of liberty by government, and antigovernment rhetoric is at times strident. On the political left, greater emphasis is placed on substantive equality among individuals and on the use of state power to help individuals who might otherwise be disadvantaged. The left sees liberty infringed by private as well as public power and often calls for government action to combat private domination. Yet whether right or left, liberal thought draws heavily on the vocabulary and mentality of individual rights. It is the individual who counts, not the community, tribe, class, or clan.

The dominance of liberalism in America has had many causes. The United States was founded at a time when the rhetoric of individual rights flourished as an antidote to political and economic oppression in Europe. America's budding liberals especially took to the writings of English philosopher John Locke, who believed that people possessed individual natural rights that arose in advance of, and hence trumped, the powers of collective governance. In the economic realm, liberalism rapidly gained ground during the first half of the nineteenth century—to the point that the state of Maine in 1843, zealously promoting individual opportunity, dropped all educational requirements for admission to the practice of law. During the century's middle decades, abolitionism and the Civil War heightened attention to civil liberties and further fueled the rhetoric of individual rights, a rhetoric that after the war shifted easily from the voting rights of former slaves to the economic liberties and laissez-faire rhetoric of big business. Since the late nineteenth century, civil rights campaigns have helped liberalism remain ascendant, from the push for woman suffrage to the minority-focused rhetoric of the late twentieth century.

Arising from and strengthening this shift toward individualism has been the influence of free-market economics and economic theory. In the worldview of the market, only individuals count, monied individuals whose preferences the market can aggregate and satisfy. As it combines the wants of individual purchasers, the market competes directly with other forms of collective action, and it has done exceedingly well in that competition. The more atomized and isolated purchasers are, the more the market can stimulate their wants and appeal to their instincts.

Market thinking has had a particularly pronounced influence on the way people think about nature. In the market, nature is divided into transferable parts—acres of land, barrels of oil, tons of ore, board feet of lumber. Parts of nature that have no market value are seen as worthless and are thus overlooked. As an organic whole, the land community can have no market value, for the whole as such cannot be bought and sold. Only discrete parts of nature, natural resources, have market value, and this value rises when they have distinct bounds—when they are clearly marked commodities that market forces can then shift to higher-priced uses. The market thus resists any form of organic vision, whether of society or of the land. In doing so, it sustains and strengthens the liberal emphasis on individuality.

The upshot of all these factors—cultural, political, and economic—has been a pronounced tendency to view the world in individual terms and to vest full moral value in the individual person, whether as market participant, voter, or private property owner. Hands down, liberty defined chiefly in negative terms—as freedom from interference in the pursuit of individual wishes, particularly freedom from collective government interference—has become the nation's central political value.

Without question, liberty has brought indispensable gains to America and the world, opening many doors that had been closed for too long. Yet like all ideas, it has its place and its limits. Sometimes these limits become plain, as they do in the land community that straddles and includes Boneyard Creek.

INTERPRETING THE BONEYARD

How does Boneyard Creek fit into this individualistic view of the world? How is this landscape interpreted in liberal, free-market terms, and how are its problems understood? And what, in turn, does the Boneyard's condition say about the prospects for achieving land health on a broader scale?

Commodities Boneyard Creek and its poorest neighborhoods face a common plight in that both are viewed by the market principally as commodities. In a market-based economy, land is considered primarily a commodity, an object that competes for market value with other land parcels near and far. As a commodity, it is like other commodities, like bricks or teacups or paper bags or pianos, something an owner can use, consume, and throw away as she or he sees fit. To gain value, the land north of the Boneyard must appeal to people who have cash to spend. In the beauty contest of the open market, local lands along the Boneyard have not fared well, particularly the many that stand vacant. Few people with cash want to buy them—for houses, stores, factories, or anything. Only nature continues to embrace these lots, covering every unpaved spot with lush weeds and sprouting trees.

The same economic system that places so little value on the empty lots north of the Boneyard also places little value on many local people. Like the land, the people are treated as market commodities. If they don't fit the market's needs, they are rejected in favor of people elsewhere who do.

Boundaries As market commodities, both land parcels and people are viewed as distinct things, separated one from the next by distinct boundaries. Such boundaries are essential to protecting the power of the individual in a liberal, free-market society. If too many links are recognized as important, individual autonomy is threatened: A laborer is no longer a distinct market participant, easily shifted from place to place; a natural resource is no longer a discrete piece of Earth, ready for the market to move around.

Along the Boneyard, fences and markers divide one urban lot from the next. To the contemporary eye, each lot appears separate in its existence, use, and management. The land, in turn, appears separate from the creek, a division that makes it hard to recognize how unnatural the Boneyard's flow regime really is. In nature, flowing water connects a waterway with its surrounding lands. Along the Boneyard, drainage work has materially distorted that connection. To the city engineer, paid to pay attention, the link is, of course, well known. To others, culturally accustomed to accepting boundaries, the relationship is obscure. When the Boneyard floods, local residents assume the problem is confined to the creek itself, to the one discrete piece of nature where it shows up. According to this view, the obvious solution is to reengineer the creek by dredging and channeling—to fix the broken piece—instead of considering watershed-wide solutions. If the connections were more visible, other solutions would become apparent, ones that allowed rainwater to percolate slowly through the soil before reaching the creek.

Values When the modern mind considers the Boneyard community, focusing on commodities and implicitly accepting boundaries, assumptions soon arise about underlying values. To such a mind, *value* means market value, measured in terms of cash equivalent. If the market doesn't place a cash value on a land parcel's produce or a person's labor, no value exists. Valueless lands lie vacant; valueless people stand idle. If a person's labor brings little or no cash return, it is worthless, and he or she might as well do nothing. Education, accordingly, means learning a skill that can be sold for cash, learning how to work for the impersonal market rather than for oneself, for friends, or for a local community. A good education is one that puts a person in a position to sell services for cash. When the market is allowed to stand as the sole measure of value, individual things soon become lumped together and viewed alike. A parcel of land in one place is the same as a parcel elsewhere if both carry the same market price. A person whose labor sells for a given price is roughly equivalent to another person whose labor sells for the same price.

The root problem with these assumptions lies in the low value often assigned to local things in their local settings. In the Boneyard, land is not valued principally for the roles it can play in sustaining local life, human and nonhuman; it is valued by and in terms of the larger organizing system that is the market economy. How does a given parcel compare with other tracts elsewhere in terms of its features and amenities? What can it produce that will compete on the market with the products of other lands, near and far? Less explicitly, the same questions are asked about the local people: How do their skills square with market needs? Can they successfully sell their services to competitive market buyers? A person from the neighborhood is deemed successful when he or she gains a marketable skill and is hired to fill a distant job. A land parcel suddenly becomes valuable when someone with cash finds it suitable for a warehouse or waste dump or when its trees or minerals or soil can be removed and sold for cash.

To value land in such traditional economic terms is to forget that land is a direct source of nourishment and shelter. In many parts of the world, the value of land continues to depend chiefly on its health. Is the soil fertile? Are the plants and animals prosperous? Is the water clean and suitable for drinking? From this perspective, value is an intensely practical concern, based on the land's lasting ability to meet life's essential needs. When food comes visibly from the surrounding soil, retaining the soil and keeping it fertile are manifest needs. When drinking water comes from a creek like the Boneyard, the cleanliness of the water becomes a vital concern, as do the cycles of flooding and drought.

Land Uses By focusing in this way on market valuation, the modern mind accepts particular ways of thinking about land uses—when land is used, how it is used, and how land uses compare with one another. When a farm field is converted to a golf course, the land has shifted in market terms from low value to high. When forest trees die and decay, in time falling with gravity, the trees have been wasted; the landowner has failed to put them to good use. When water in an arid land is allowed to flow into the sea, uninterrupted by irrigators and thirsty cities, its use has been inefficient.

In contrast, from an ecological perspective, land is always in use, often in ways essential to the maintenance of its health. A dying tree is profitably used when it supplies food and shelter to birds, particularly when the birds eat insects that would otherwise damage food crops. A wetland is actively used when it retains storm water, thereby regulating flooding, limiting siltation, and keeping water supplies secure. From this holistic view, a mole uses topsoil to grow earthworms for dinner. The soil uses dead plants and animals to regain its fertility. Far from being wasted or useless, water left in a stream helps sustain fish and other aquatic life.

The Social Order In the ideology of the free market, a human community is little more than a collection of individuals who interact in the market. Each consumer is a separate actor in aggressive pursuit of personal wants; each worker is an independent laborer selling services to the highest bidder. Such free-market thinking appeals to many Americans because the individual is so central to it. It exalts individual freedom and downplays countervailing ideas of interconnectedness and interdependence.

When the human community is broken into parts in this manner, the links among people become easily overlooked, just as they do when nature is divided. Individuals are valued separately, and responsibility is assigned largely at the individual level. When residents along the Boneyard encounter troubles, the diagnosis rarely points to the lack of a strong local social fabric and neighborhood-based economic enterprises. The problem is alleviated when a local resident, or two or five, gets enough training to gain employment in a market job, most likely somewhere else. It is the individual piece—the individual person—that needs repair, whether through additional training, medical treatment, or simply a better attitude.

Other types of repair—the social equivalent of the Boneyard's watershed plan—are often pushed to the side and made harder to perceive.

The Missing Senses When a modern mind examines an inhabited landscape through the lens of an individualistic, market-oriented world, it discounts the senses in which the whole is more than its parts. Lost are certain vital understandings about the land and its people:

- The sense that a local community is part of a natural ecosystem, with the health and productivity of the local land tied to and undergirding human health and productivity
- The sense that the local community is more than a haphazard collection of individuals; it is a place populated by families, tribes, clans, neighborhoods, congregations, towns, clubs, business entities, and the like—acting not in isolation but in concert and within a unifying context
- The sense that the land can directly support the people who live on it, to meet their needs for food, fuel, and shelter
- The sense that people with diverse skills, adapted to a locale, can go a long way toward meeting their basic needs by working for themselves and their families and by sharing and exchanging with their neighbors
- The senses of accomplishment, pleasure, independence, and dignity that arise when a person relies on the self rather than on others to grow food and meet other essential needs

A SECOND LOOK

A culture that exalts individualism does not willingly embrace the communal values so necessary to the promotion of land health. Collective action is looked on with suspicion, and so, too, is any substantive conception of the common good. Individuals are allowed to do as they please as long as they respect the equal rights

of others. Words such as *cooperation, sharing,* and *trust* still have a
place, but they become voluntary virtues, things people do if they
choose. Community membership also becomes a voluntary matter—if people want to join a community, they may, but participation is optional.

From this perspective, the goal of land health is awkward and
troubling. The concept of land health builds on the ecological reality that people who live in a place are necessarily part of the resident community. Together, they form a whole that is far more than
the sum of the parts, and the health of that whole is a communal
good, achievable only through collective action. Membership in
the community is assigned to each person who lives in a place; it is
not something a person can choose or refuse at will.

Another obstacle to promoting land health in an individualistic
world is the tendency for confrontation rather than cooperation.
Individuals are expected to represent themselves, pursue their own
interests, and make deals with other people. When tension arises,
the rhetoric commonly used is one of antagonism. Sometimes it's
the rhetoric of individual rights: Party A points to a right to life;
party B points to a right to choice. Sometimes it's the rhetoric of
negotiation or courtroom drama, with A arguing one side and B
arguing the other. In each case parties are advocates, each side
pushing hard until resistance is met and compromise is reached or
a ruling is made. Out of clashes of self-set interests, communal life
takes shape.

This mode of interaction is simply not conducive to the promotion of land health. The rhetoric of competing interests accentu-
ates boundaries and separateness and casts participants as opponents. A seller demands a high price; a buyer insists on a low one.
In the case of land health, however, there are no such opposing
sides, however much people might differ in their visions of what
land health means. The land's health is a single condition, and each
local resident is intertwined with it. Although people can debate

what constitutes land health and how it may be achieved, in the end a truly healthy land can arise only from cooperation and shared values.

Before the liberal tradition gained such strength, people thought of themselves far more in social terms, with their fates tied to the strengths of their social institutions—their families, tribes, churches, local communities, and the like. If people weren't taught it, they soon learned from experience that they needed to cooperate with one another if they expected to survive. In this moral order, the responsible individual was the person who kept an eye on the collective good even while pursuing separate aims.

To promote land health, modern culture needs to revisit some of the social mores of the past. Older ideas need to return, ethical views that honored the person who worked for the common good—in this case, the good of the land community. A fully ethical person needs to recognize the value of that community, to know about the links that are vital to it, and to step forward to help nourish those links. Modern culture also needs to place a higher value on communal decision making. By viewing individuals in isolation and exalting their freedom of choice, modern thought encourages people to think only of themselves and to make decisions alone.

In its original form, liberalism sought not only to promote the individual as such but also to vest individuals with the power to join with others to pursue shared aims. By acting jointly, people could achieve goals that were out of reach for them when they acted alone. Collective action, of course, is possible today, but it usually requires the consent of all participants. The requirement of full consent does empower people by allowing them to say no, but it also weakens them, particularly when they seek goals that are achievable only if everyone joins in. Land health is a prime example of such a goal. Individual rights shouldn't be elevated to the point at which people are denied the chance to deal collectively with vital problems.

A related intellectual tradition that also needs to regain strength is the tradition recognizing the rights of communities. In antebellum America, while Maine was rushing to open its bar to any person of good moral character, however illiterate, a separate tradition continued to thrive in public discourse and judicial decision making. This was the tradition that spoke of the "well-ordered" society and of rights a community could assert to keep individual behavior in check. A celebrated judicial opinion that drew upon this tradition came in the case of *Commonwealth v. Alger*, authored in 1851 by Chief Justice Lemuel Shaw of the Massachusetts Supreme Judicial Court.

In *Alger*, the court considered a state statute that banned landowners along Boston harbor from building wharves that extended so far into the harbor that navigation was endangered. Cyrus Alger built a wharf in violation of the law and when prosecuted, he claimed that the law interfered with his private rights. The court upheld Alger's prosecution, and in doing so it emphasized that communal interests outweighed private rights. In a "well ordered civil society," Justice Shaw wrote, the use of private property must not be injurious either to other property owners or to "the rights of the community." Property rights were held subject to reasonable regulation, including regulations that promoted "the common good and general welfare." A few years earlier, a New York court had made a similar pronouncement: "The sovereign power in a community, therefore, may and ought to prescribe the manner of exercising individual rights over property . . . [so that] the benefit of all is promoted. . . . Such power is incident to every well regulated society."

As the nineteenth century progressed, language about community rights tended to appear less often in court reports and in public discourse. Over time, rights came to mean, pretty much by definition, individual rights. That slippage occurred for various reasons, an important one being people's decreased confidence in identifying the good of the community as opposed to the good of interest groups that pressed the government for particular laws and programs.

Today, to the modern mind contemplating the Boneyard, there is little sense that the land and its people form a community that might have rights and might have a "common good" distinguishable from the good of individuals, the kind of common good, for instance, that is ill served by shipping its most able young people to jobs far away. If the Boneyard region were seen as a community and not a commodity, if the modern mind could recapture the desirability of maintaining here a "well-ordered" society, the promotion of land health would make ready sense. It would fit together easily with other goals related to the ordering and healthy functioning of the community's internal processes.

Chapter 5

Mat Feltner's World

For many readers, Kentucky farmer and writer Wendell Berry has become America's preeminent writer of place. In an era of mobility, Berry writes about staying put and sinking roots. At a time when critics blame problems on big business and corrupt politics, Berry looks inward to the human soul, probing its flaws and possibilities. As concerned as anyone about sagging land health, he has never considered the issue apart from the long-term health of people. Indeed, he has never separated the welfare of the land community from the ways in which people have succeeded and failed in their efforts to live sensibly at home.

Berry is much admired for his essays and poetry, yet many readers find his mind and heart most vividly at work in his novels and short stories. All are set in a fictionalized version of Berry's home country, renamed Port William, along the Kentucky River just south of the Ohio. In his fiction, Berry recounts the lives of several interconnected farm families over the course of the past century. As he does so, he probes many of the challenges of twentieth-century life, including the central challenge of using the land without abusing it. In the failings of Berry's characters, one recognizes the failings of modern culture; in their successes, one sees the possibilities of hope.

In his story, "The Boundary," Berry writes about the life of one of his favorite characters, Mat Feltner. A dependable, honorable man, Mat has enjoyed a long and successful marriage to his hilly, demanding farm and to the community of people who surround him. On the day of the story, set in the 1960s, Mat's life is nearing its end. Knowingly, willingly, he approaches the boundary that separates him and those who will continue after him from the many acquaintances he has among the dead. On this day, weak though he is, Mat gets the urge to inspect the barbed-wire fence that surrounds his rugged farm. The fence, he worries, might have fallen into disrepair; the younger men, rushing to get the harvest in, might have been too busy to check the fence and mend it. So, cane in hand, Mat sets out to inspect his physical boundary, with a weariness in his bones that for the moment he seems to shake.

Crossing his field, Mat travels into the woods and down a long ravine. As he walks and inspects, Mat considers what this farm has meant to him for eight decades, what it meant to the people who came before him here, and what it will mean to those who follow. He reminds himself, fondly and easily, of the endless fascination this particular farm has provided him. As his memories take over, Mat recalls the day seventy-five years earlier when, as a boy, he accompanied his father and the work crew that installed the wire fence. It is a warm memory, and Mat lingers on it. Soon the scene shifts: It is forty years later, and Mat has taken charge, leading to the same place a work crew that includes his own son. The two scenes, we note, are remarkably similar. The ways of living and enjoying the land have changed little over the decades; the continuities of manners and means roll on with the years. Time continues to swirl in Mat's mind and he is reminded, again and again, of the work that has been done on the farm and of the people who have mixed their lives with the place. Most of them are dead now, at rest on a hill not far away, yet Mat senses their presence beside him. Transcending death, they have retained their membership in the local community; they remain present in the enduring memories of the living and in the communal wisdom they nourished and passed down.

Checking the fence, Mat soon realizes that he had no need to fear. The younger men have not been too busy to care for it. The needed work has been done and done well, just as Mat would have done it years earlier and as Mat's father, Ben, would have done it before him, the generations securely linked in a tradition of good work and attentive devotion. Warmed by these thoughts, Mat struggles on, his strength ebbing as the terrain becomes more rugged. His path has taken him, he realizes, to a place where he has trouble continuing on. Yet he refuses to give in. His life has not been about giving in. "He chooses," as he always has, "the difficult familiar way." He is not ready to cross the boundary into death.

As the day wears on, Mat realizes that his wife, Margaret, will have missed him and become worried. He thinks, too, of the younger men at work in the hayfield a ridge or two away—what they will be doing at that time of day, how they will be doing it, and the feelings that will inhabit them. So similar are their lives, so intertwined are their ways, that the members of this community give rise to something greater than what they are as individuals. The land is part of them, and they are part of it. There is a unity here that is felt powerfully, a wholeness that radiates in health, contentment, and beauty.

Tired though he is, Mat nonetheless carries on:

A shadowless love moves him now, not his, but a love that he belongs to, as he belongs to the place and to the light over it. He is thinking of Margaret and of all that his plighting with her has led to. He is thinking of the membership of the fields that he has belonged to all his life, and will belong to while he breathes, and afterward. He is thinking of the living ones of that membership – at work in the fields that the dead were at work in before them.

Reaching the crest, Mat rests against a large walnut tree that "stands alone outside the woods." There he will soon be found and helped home by younger members who partake of this same love. As we watch Mat lean against the tree, we sense how like the tree he has become. They are kindred spirits, the two of them, roughly equal in age and coming, finally, to the same spot. By the life he has led, standing erect in the light, Mat, too, has stood "outside the woods." Just as the walnut has relinquished its seeds, so Mat has given freely of himself, nourishing the land and giving rise to new life. Like the tree, Mat has sunk deep and lasting roots. And as the tree in time will do, Mat will die and become one again with the native soil.

OWNING, CARING, AND BELONGING

"The Boundary" is a lyrical, moving tale, a love story of people and place. The story has to do with the mending of a fence, as Frost's "Mending Wall" does, yet the fence again supplies merely the setting for the unfolding drama. Mixed in with that drama are useful lessons about land ethics and the good ways in which people and land can come together. As Mat walks the bounds of his chosen farm, probably for the last time, he recalls the exact terrain that has been the focus of his life. His fence, that is, marks not only the boundary of his farm but also the boundary of his particularized love. With this farm he has mixed his labor, hard labor and plenty of it. Attentive to its many limits—its slopes, its fragile soils, its vital springs—he has wooed the farm with care. Married to it, he has forsaken all other lands; mixing his manhood with it, he has made it yield.

In "The Boundary," Berry gives a view of land division rarely seen in contemporary writing, particularly in writing by authors so cognizant of the land's degradation. For Mat Feltner and others, boundaries offer positive virtues. They mark out lines of responsibility. They allow for a special love between owner and soil. They nourish a special sense of continuity across generations, fostering greater attention to those who will inherit the land and depend on its productivity. A vital element of this continuity, Berry reveals, is the preserving and enhancing of special knowledge about a given place, the kind of local, practical knowledge that can separate the sensitive land use from the unintentionally abusive one. Mat Feltner learned to respect his farm from his father and others. Over the years, he has preserved that vital fund of knowledge and added to it. He has fulfilled his stewardship duties to the human community as well as to the land, conveying freely to younger members the wisdom that he knows is not just his.

Mat's attitude toward his land contrasts starkly with the liberal, free-market view of modern culture. Although his land is his economic base, Mat doesn't perceive the farm simply as a commodity as so many others do, and his understanding of the concept of "economy" includes more than market transactions. The farm, to begin with, is the Feltners' home, the place where Mat and his family have chosen to live. As they've lived there, decade on decade, the place has become inseparable from the family itself. By working the land, Mat has shaped it in ways that show his artistry as a farmer. The land has become an object of beauty, yielding aesthetic benefits that never show up on any balance sheet or tax return. The produce of the Feltner farm is intentionally varied. Along with farm animals and crops raised for market, there are the many crops raised for family use, from garden vegetables to berry bushes to woodlot trees supplying firewood and lumber. The land's recreational value is another product, never marketed and probably not marketable but valuable all the same to the Feltners and their guests.

It is evident, given these varied products and the intimacy here between people and land, that Mat Feltner has uncommon ideas about land value and land use. He is not insensitive to crop prices and to cash income, given the taxes he pays and the items he necessarily buys, but Mat's understanding of value is only indirectly linked to the market. Value has to do with the condition of the farm, its fertility, good order, and beauty. Are the fields laid out to yield good crops while retaining the soil? Are crop rotations scheduled so that pests are kept in check and clover or other green manure is regularly turned under? Are livestock pastures arranged and fenced so that overgrazing is avoided and stream banks are not eroded by hooves? Is there a freshwater spring on the farm, one that flows reliably even in the driest of weather? Is waste properly composted so that the cycle of fertility remains intact? Above all, is there a sense of rightful proportion on the farm, a sense that the proper amount of land is devoted to each of the farm's activities—pasture, row crops, woodlot, garden, flowers, homestead?

As Mat walks his fence line, he thinks as much about the human community as he does about the land. On a nearby ridge, younger people are at work—neighbors and friends who perform certain tasks collectively, making their work more pleasant as they reaffirm their ties. While the men work the fields, the women and children are probably interacting as well, perhaps preparing food, perhaps working in gardens or performing other chores. It is not simply the living people, however, who compose this social order. The dead are there, too, vividly so for a community member as close to death as Mat. The present generations join hands with past ones, just as neighbor is linked to neighbor. The connections, of course, vary in strength. Some residents never fit into the community particularly well. But they partake of the membership nonetheless because every local resident by definition is included.

Given Mat's orientation to the land, one might easily imagine his reaction if he were to visit Boneyard Creek. Instinctively he would compare this creek with others, creeks in which the water flowed clearly, wildlife abounded, and native trees supplied shade. Mat would dislike the Boneyard, not because he was shocked by it but because it exemplified so much of what he opposed. He would see there an inattentiveness to the land's natural features and processes. He would see painful evidence of sloppy work, misguided hopes, and bad values. A creek that might have served many uses is devoted, unwisely, to merely one: a public sewer. A creek that local people might have known intimately and appreciated aesthetically, recreationally, and spiritually has taken on a crude, instrumental role.

As Mat viewed the Boneyard's people, he might react less with anger than with sadness at the lost opportunities, misguided faith, and wasted talent. Although he would grope for answers to many questions, he might wonder mostly why the people haven't recognized what they possess and made better use of it. With so many vacant lots, why are there no gardens? With soil so rich, why are there no fruit trees? With buildings unused, why are there no handicraft operations, organized not to produce market goods but to meet directly the needs of local people? Where, in short, are the sense of attachment to the land and the spirit of sharing and cooperation?

Of the various elements that make up the environmental critique, few seem to apply to Mat Feltner's ways of thinking and living. If he has missed many of the benefits of the modern age, he has missed many of its ailments, too. Mat's knowledge of the land comes as much from intuition and long-developing sentiment as it does from empirical sensory perceptions of the rational modern mind. There is an aura about him, an ethical sensibility or attachment to virtue, that displays respect for other life-forms and a willingness to make room for them. Mat's ethical reasoning overtly includes future generations as well as respecting departed ones; in this regard, too, Mat deviates from the modern mind's focus on the present. Finally, everything around him, including the people, form in his mind an organic whole. The people live with the animals, the animals with the plants, and all depend ultimately upon sunlight, water, and soil for nourishment and health. Mat's view is not exactly biocentric; humans still count for more. Yet he has softened markedly the human/nature dualism. Humans are special creatures, yet they are as thoroughly rooted in nature as any other creature.

As a farmer who provides first for his family's sustenance and only then for the market, Mat thinks of his land in complex terms. He knows the land intimately, what can be done with it and how far it can be pushed. He knows, too, that he cannot accomplish what he does without the help of family and friends, a supporting network of people who are also attached to this place. Embedded as he is, Mat embraces a view of his surroundings that is distinctly ecological. Every piece is connected to every other piece, forming an interdependent whole. Mat uses this whole, as he must, yet he respects it as he uses it, with humility and with love.

LESSONS FROM PORT WILLIAM

In Mat Feltner, Wendell Berry presents his ideal farmer and citizen; not a flawless man, but as close to it as humans normally come. Feltner's values and understandings are ones that Berry himself embraces. In offering Feltner to the world, Berry has, of course, many literary aims, including the desire to preserve faithfully his memories of whatever man or men served as models for the fictional patriarch. Yet he aims also to present an agrarian alternative to modern ways of interpreting and dwelling on the land. In this way, Mat Feltner becomes a teacher, endowed with an uncommon array of admirable traits. He is also an extraordinary citizen, righteous, sociable, devoted, talented. Another man, living in the same house and tilling the same land, might not match Mat's success. Still, apart from his good character, there are elements of Mat Feltner's world that have helped make his success possible, elements from which other people and other communities might learn.

To begin with, Feltner's way of farming is specifically tailored to the hilly, humid lands of north-central Kentucky, as it should be. Moreover, the Feltner family lives simply, and its economic security depends on that simplicity. Berry doesn't reveal the financial details of the Feltners' farm, yet money is readily available when children head to school and friends need loans. Given his economic security, Mat can dream about his land because he has no worries about losing it, legally or economically. He can think not only of his lifetime but also of generations yet to come on his farm, generations he hopes will include his descendants or, short of that, other young people who have proven themselves worthy. Would Mat behave differently if his land title were insecure? Surely he would invest less of himself in the place, be more inclined to push the land to its limits, exhaust the soil, log the woodlot, and ignore erosion.

Mat Feltner's sense of security and longevity arises in part because his farm is his private property. Indirectly in "The Boundary" and more overtly in other writings, Wendell Berry speaks highly of private landownership. Such ownership, he notes, supplies an incentive to care and gives rise to some of the most useful metaphors of stewardship and attachment to place. In Berry's fictional landscape, tenant farmers rarely have Feltner's devotion, for they lack the indispensable tenure that fosters lasting devotion. As Berry argues in one of his essays, the word "property" "always implies the intimate involvement of a proprietary mind—not the mind of ownership, as that term is necessarily defined by the industrial economy, but a mind possessed of the knowledge, affection, and skill appropriate to the keeping and use of its property." The essential point, Berry cautions, is that "land cannot be properly cared for by people who do not know it intimately, who do not know how to care for it, who are not strongly motivated to care for it, and who cannot afford to care for it." Given these constraints, proper landownership can occur only when land is divided into human-sized pieces and used on such a scale that all work is the product of a "proprietary mind." Mat Feltner succeeded because his farm was small enough for him to know intimately. Had he taken on more acres, hiring tenants to work on his behalf, his land surely would have suffered.

And then there is the matter of Mat's human community. From others, he learned how to farm his land, both the particulars of using his chosen farm and the more general attitudes and values that guide the farming operation. There was in Mat's community what Berry likes to call a "handing down" of local knowledge from one generation to the next and one neighbor to another. No single generation, much less a single farm family, could have learned what the community now knows. It is perhaps the community's most valuable asset.

Mat Feltner's community, though, does more than offer him its wisdom. It calls him to participate responsibly in its existence and continuation. It sets expectations and instills feelings of obligation. Mat is well aware of his indebtedness to those who taught him. And he knows, too, that he can never repay them directly, no matter how devoted he is to their memory. He can repay only by husbanding the communal wisdom and adding to it as best he can and, when the chance arises, imparting that wisdom to the next generation. It is a form of repayment that mimics the cycles of nature rather than the bargained reciprocity of contracts.

Of Wendell Berry's many contributions, perhaps none is more valuable than his portrayal of how good land use can reliably occur only in communities that value it and are structured to encourage and help sustain it. Even Mat Feltner, knowledgeable and dedicated as he is, succeeded only because he stood on others' shoulders. If other landowners are to repeat Mat's success, they, too, will need advantages like his. This focus on community sets Berry apart from Aldo Leopold. Like Berry, Leopold honored the responsible, ethical landowner, yet he didn't appreciate, or at least didn't emphasize, the need for communal support for the individual owner who wanted to embrace a healthier land ethic. Leopold, an expert ecologist, was able to use his own worn-out farm in ways that gradually moved it back toward health, although even he had his share of failures. Less knowledgeable landowners plainly would need help.

Finally, in the assessment of Mat Feltner's success, there is the matter of boundaries and what they have meant in Mat's life and mind. Mat's fence is the boundary that contains his livestock and marks the limits of his particularized affection. On Mat's mind as he walks is a second boundary, nearer every day, that separates the living from the dead. There are also the boundaries that separate Mat from his family and his family from neighbors and the community at large. There is the boundary that separates humans from other animals, and there is the boundary, cognizant to the religious mind, that separates the Creation from the Creator.

These boundaries are important in "The Boundary" and in the rest of Berry's writing. As readers, we are tempted to think that boundaries are secure, exemplified most visibly by the barbed-wire fence. Yet at closer reading, this boundary is not as firm as it appears, nor are the others. Mat's fence may contain farm animals but it contains little else. Mat's neighbors have no trouble crossing it to visit, nor does Mat himself, physically or mentally. Other animals pass over and under it, as do the wind and the rain. Mat's heart is focused on this farm, but he is plainly aware of what goes on elsewhere, particularly what other farm families are doing. In spare moments, he roams the familiar countryside and enjoys its natural splendors.

The other boundaries in Mat's life are also permeable ones, and their permeability has a lot to do with Mat's success. In Port William, those who die nonetheless live on, as memories and in stories, in the wisdom they've handed down, and in the local lands that reflect their handiwork. Living people are connected not only to the dead but also to the unborn, whose coming is anticipated and in whose name much work is done. Mat is his own man, as Berry reveals, yet his orientation has always been toward his family, near and far, and his family in turn has blended with other community members. Mat has stood by his neighbors in times of need, sacrificing for them as if they were kin. Living as close as he does to other animals and the land, Mat feels tied to the natural order in a way few city dwellers can ever imagine.

Finally, there is the boundary, so important in Berry's writing, that separates Mat and his farm from Earth's Creator. To Berry's religious mind, the Creation is an ongoing process and tillers of the soil take part in it: They are included within the Creation, yet through their work the creative process unfolds. Like other good farmers, Mat Feltner works hard to sustain the essential cycle of fertility by which the living return to the soil to decay, passing through darkness and then rising up, resurrected, into new life. Earthly life depends on the soundness of this cycle, and farmers who maintain it engage creatively in worship and praise. Thus, by tending the garden, Mat honors Earth as Creation and unites himself, insofar as he can, with the Creator.

Paradoxically, then, a story that seems at first to honor the taut, fenced boundary is very much about a man who has transcended boundaries, many of them, and has lived a better life because of it. Mat's farming didn't succeed because he stood apart from his land. He didn't develop his skills by keeping a fence between himself and his neighbors. His farm didn't become healthy because he thought only of the present. Mat never sought to erase these boundaries, but boundaries were never firm or rigid in his intuitively ecological view. Life flowed through them, and so did responsibilities.

PORT WILLIAM'S LIMITS

Wendell Berry is too honest a writer to pretend that all farmers in Port William are like Mat Feltner. The best ones are, and others are nearly as good. But many have drifted into the kind of present-oriented, profit-driven farming practices that prove destructive.

Berry knows this reality well, for when he returned to his ancestral Kentucky home in the mid-1960s, he took up residence on a small farm so thoroughly abused that for years no one had tried to farm it. The hillside was badly eroded. Buildings were abandoned. Fences were in disrepair. Berry draws on this history in his fiction and, even more critically, in his essays. Port William has its share of farmers who abuse the land.

If all landowners were like Mat Feltner, Berry's vision would indeed be persuasive. But one wonders what Port William can do with farmers who don't live up to Mat's high standards. In real life, wouldn't such a community be dragged down by members who don't do their share? Wouldn't the work of handing down sometimes wither for lack of good people to carry it on? And if some farmers were willing to abuse land to boost profits, wouldn't the Feltner types feel pressure to take shortcuts as well? Can Port William, in short, get by with such informal, voluntary mechanisms to express and enforce its expectations?

One wonders, too, whether Mat Feltner, sensitive though he is, can really satisfy the ecological needs of the landscape that includes his farm. As he tends his land, does Mat consider the ecosystem processes that sustain his home region? Does he provide adequate room for resident plant and animal species? Are his drainage practices consistent with prevention of downstream flooding? However noble are Mat's motives, does he really know enough to foster the health of the organic whole? And even if he does, how many other farmers do as well?

Mat Feltner's example is also limited because his farming methods are so unusual, a holdover from a mostly bygone era. Mat farms in ways that prevailed before modern chemicals and bioengineering entered the scene. He can still afford to use natural fertilizers and leave acres fallow or in pasture every year. But will his descendants be able to do the same? The wisdom of the generations could prove inadequate to the pressures of low crop prices, high-tech production methods, and international free trade. From his father, his Uncle Jack, and others, Mat learned about draft horses but nothing about pesticide application methods, bioengineered seeds, or wetland restoration techniques.

A further problem, aggravated by industrial technology, is that bad farmers now have more potent ways to degrade the land than when, like Mat Feltner, they used draft horses for traction and manures for fertilizer. The insensitive farmer no longer diminishes just his own farm, as disastrous as that may be. His chemicals percolate into the groundwater, which ends up in the Feltner family well. Behind the wheel of a huge tractor, a single farmer can till ten times the acreage Mat ever could, causing more erosion in one year than Mat's worst neighbor did in a decade. In Mat's day, Port William could count on bad farmers going under economically before too much damage was done. Now, that margin of error is gone.

PRIVATE LAND

"The Boundary" is, among other things, a valuable addition to the fund of narratives dealing with the private ownership of land. Like other literary writers, Berry contributes to this fund not with an abstract assessment of the subject—a tale of a nameless owner and a hypothetical tract of land—but with a case study depicting a fleshed-out owner dwelling on a well-described piece of land. In Mat Feltner's world, property ownership tethers a family to the land in ways that encourage familiarity and devotion, and it provides the foundation for enduring, land-enhancing human communities.

Berry's narrative of private landownership is especially useful because it shows the possible benefits of an institution that many environmentalists rightly view with suspicion. In the eyes of many, private property ownership stands alongside individualism and the free market as a potent obstacle to the pursuit of land health. Mat

Feltner might have viewed his land boundaries as permeable ones, but the law that sanctioned his ownership treated them more concretely. The local police recognized Mat's boundaries and protected him from trespassers. At law, Mat was largely free to use his land as he liked, and he could have exercised that freedom by ruining his farm. The dark side of landownership is that it protects and sanctions activities that degrade the land, making remedial work all the more cumbersome and expensive.

The question that surrounds private property ownership, then, is whether it is sufficiently flexible as an institution that its good elements can be retained while its weak ones are somehow pruned. Can property law be reshaped to better promote land health without disrupting its other important aims, its roles in maintaining a sound civic order, protecting privacy, and promoting economic enterprise? Could property law have stimulated the enterprise of California's mining camps without degrading nearby rivers? Could it have fostered Mat Feltner's devotion without allowing his neighbors to drag the region down with their exploitive activities?

Private landownership is inherently a flexible institution, capable of taking many forms and promoting various ends. But it is more than just a useful institution. It has symbolic functions as well, and efforts to reshape it in the name of land health need to begin by recognizing those functions. Particularly in America, private property ownership is intimately intertwined with the nation's identity as a land of liberty, democracy, and economic growth. It also undergirds the self-identities of landowners as independent, proud individuals. Private ownership of land has been a central part of the story of America since its founding—a story about settling the land and creating a beacon of freedom to shine around the world.

Efforts to reshape property law need to come to grips with these vital symbolic roles. Healthier landownership norms—ones that promote a better sense of community—somehow need to fit into the dominant visions of America. Laws that promote land health need to fit together with the self-identities of landowners in a way that ordinary people can understand and embrace.

Thus, the task that lies ahead in reshaping property law is a large one indeed, and work is needed at various levels, from crafting the most detailed land-use rules to reimagining how land-use limits might fit into the dominant American ethos. In "The Boundary" and other writings, Wendell Berry has materially aided the broad-scale work, the work needed at the level of symbolism and imagination. In Mat Feltner, we have one example of what the American land very much needs: an independent, distinctly American landowner who respects the land and works for the common good.

Chapter 6

Private Property and the American Dream

IN RECENT YEARS, landowners such as rancher Clayton Williams have wielded private property rights as a shield against unwanted restraints, particularly environmental land-use laws. Williams's complaint, filed in federal district court, was necessarily written by lawyers and framed in legal terms. Had Williams been free to tell his own tale, his words might have taken a different form. His story might have begun generations earlier, when settlers first entered Wyoming's harsh high plateau. He might have told about the spirit of independence that propelled people there, a yearning for open space and fewer constraints. Whatever its exact shape, the story would probably be about maverick spirits seeking lives with more wildness and less domesticity. Yet despite this yearning for wildness, secure private property ownership would be part of the story, as it was part of Mat Feltner's. Boundaries were needed to keep other people away while owners carved homes out of the raw landscape.

Frontier narratives of wildness are as common in American culture as tales of pastoral domesticity: the independence of Wyoming ranch country on one side; the settled embeddedness of Port William, Kentucky, on the other. Few storytellers have captured these contrasting stories as well as Wallace Stegner, whose novel *The Big Rock Candy Mountain* brings them together in the form of an energetic young couple, Bo and Elsa Mason. From settled Iowa, the Masons head west and north early in the twentieth century to the still-unbroken plains of southern Saskatchewan, Canada. Not finding there the prosperity they seek, they drift south to the Dakotas and then west again to Utah. In Bo Mason, Stegner portrays the wanderlust and conquering urges that showed up so often on the American frontier. Resistant to laws, Bo yearns to get rich quick, to find his Big Rock Candy Mountain. Bo's wife, Elsa, carries forward the far different spirit of domesticity. As resistant to each move as Bo is eager, she desires rootedness, not independence, health rather than wealth. Wallace Stegner understood the power of myth and the central role private landownership played in so many of America's myths. He knew, as his onetime student Wendell Berry came to know, that a well-settled American culture requires good narratives to help bring it about and sustain it.

Clayton Williams's legal claim fits into the storytelling tradition about people and place that includes Frost, Berry, Stegner, and so many others. But to grasp Williams's perspective properly, one must consider it alongside other tales that deal with the American land and the ways in which people, land, and property ownership fit together. In America, settlers began thinking about land and landownership the moment they stepped ashore, seeking to make sense of the unexplored continent and to figure out their role on it.

Americans' focus on boundaries and working the land has continued ever since, framing societal attitudes toward private property ownership to the present day.

TALES OF EDEN, OLD AND NEW

As the first colonists went about their backbreaking work, they instinctively turned to the Bible to supply meaning and context for their lives. For some of them, the New World was a promised land, not unlike the land Moses sought in the Exodus. For John Winthrop and his band of Puritans, New England was the place God had chosen for them to erect their city on a hill that their light might shine forth in accordance with the Sermon on the Mount. Over and over, though, it was the Book of Genesis, and, within Genesis, the story of Adam and Eve in the Garden of Eden that gave the colonists a sense of what they were about.

The Eden narrative fascinated the colonists just as it had caught the interest of generations before them. Their fascination arose, paradoxically, as much from the story's ambiguity and malleability as from its importance. The Eden story wasn't so much a single tale as a collection of raw materials from which several tales might arise. One narrative that took root likened the New World to the Garden of Eden itself. Just as Adam and Eve had been placed in Eden, so, too, were the colonists led to America. It was a lush, fertile land, this America, so wonderfully designed and so abundant in its yield that the colonists' needs would be met forever. In this interpretive myth, America was a friendly, productive place. The unbroken forests represented wealth, as did the rivers teeming with fish. To enjoy this garden, the colonists needed merely to live in it, in as godly a way as they knew how.

Alongside this America-as-Eden narrative grew a second, much different one. In this alternative story, America wasn't Eden; it was the wilderness to which Adam and Eve had been banished when they misbehaved. Now, this wilderness had much potential, but the colonists needed to transform it with their labor, taming it and controlling it, before the land would be habitable. In this story, the ideal garden was not the unaltered land that greeted the colonists when they first arrived but rather the well-tended, pastoral countryside around a New England village or a Virginia plantation. Trees had to be cut, the land plowed, fences erected, and wild beasts driven off before Eden would rise again.

This second narrative diminished the luster of the raw New World, but it comported better with the realities of hardworking frontier life. It also fit well with the institution of private landownership, so important in the colonists' lives. Adam and Eve might have frolicked and gamboled, feeding on grapes at their leisure, but colonists had to work hard for their bread. And they didn't want to work without knowing they could reliably harvest what they planted. They wanted, that is, their own private property. Back in England, land had been hard to get. In the New World, land was plentiful, and few colonists were content to go without. By the time of the Revolution, colonial culture had changed markedly, and the economy had changed along with it. Individualism had become much stronger, and nature was increasingly viewed as a collection of natural resources rather than a mysterious, organic whole. In the economic realm, more and more farming was done to produce surplus crops or livestock for the market rather than food for home consumption. A true market economy was rapidly developing. To Americans wrapped up in this change, John Locke's writings made a good deal of sense. Locke celebrated the common individual, arguing that he possessed natural rights that existed independently of the state and that trumped even the powers of the king. Preeminent among those rights was the right to own property. As Locke interpreted the Bible, God originally gave Earth to humankind as collective property, yet any individual could seize a piece of land from the common stock and make it his own simply by mixing labor with it. Before labor was added, the land had no value. Once labor was applied, however, value arose and the tilled land become private property.

Locke's theory of property ownership made particularly good sense in North America, more so than in England. Frontier colonists could readily agree that labor was essential to the creation of value. Moreover, because land was plentiful, one person's occupation of land didn't deny others the chance to gain land, too. By contrast, in England a person had to buy property or inherit it, and one person's occupation of land did limit another's chance to do the same.

Americans instinctively linked Locke's theory of property ownership to the second interpretation of the Garden of Eden story, the narrative of progress in which labor transformed the dangerous wilderness into a peaceful, pastoral garden. North America was the raw land described by Locke, waiting to be seized. By laboring on it, the colonists gained property rights at the same time that they transformed the land into the new Eden. Private land-ownership, it turned out, was a highly effective engine of progress, providing just the incentive needed to induce the rebuilding of paradise.

Eventually, this progressive story of human labor taming the wilderness overshadowed the first interpretation of the Eden story, which valued more highly the untouched land. Thomas Jefferson kept alive this first narrative when he defended the beauty and perfection of North America to his doubtful European correspondents. And by the time Jefferson died, in 1826, the first tradition was enjoying renewed favor among romantic writers, who looked to nature for meaning and inspiration. But writers were an elite few, and it wasn't until the end of the nineteenth century that this interpretation regained much support. By then, the frontier era had ended and people were beginning to mourn the loss of wild places. Outdoor hiking and camping became the rage as people sought to regain contact with the dwindling wilds. The Boy Scouts of America and Camp Fire organization (now the Camp Fire Boys and Girls) were founded. John Muir regaled readers with his adventures in the Sierra Nevada and Alaska and gained a rapt audience when he spoke of the inherent value of wildlands. In *The Call of the Wild*, Jack London captured the public imagination with his tale of a domestic dog that joined the wolves. Then there was the true blockbuster of the day, the captivating tale of an English infant reared in the jungle, *Tarzan of the Apes*.

By the late nineteenth century the altered American landscape itself had become more ambiguous in its messages, just like the Eden story in Genesis. Labor could indeed add value to the land and make it more productive, just as John Locke said it did. But land also had value without labor, and it was becoming clear that too much labor could be as bad as too little. When misapplied, labor could bring ruin to the land, scraping away trees, eroding soil, and polluting waters. To alter the wilderness was sometimes to bring not progress but decline.

As the countryside showed more scars of misuse, this declensional interpretation made greater sense to people, prompting calls for conservation, pollution control, and preservation of wildlife refuges and wilderness areas. Conservation measures became more numerous, placing limits on the expanding market economy that Locke's reasoning had helped propel. At the same time, ethical attitudes toward the land were shifting. To see inherent value in the land, as John Muir and others were doing, was to reaffirm that humans alone had not created all value. If the land had been a fruitful garden before people entered it, then people were merely tenders of that garden subject to divine instructions, and the private property rights they held were limited accordingly. This way of thinking represented a demotion in status for people, from conquerors and creators of value to something less than that, stewards of value that already existed, shepherds of animals and plants lent to humankind in trust.

OVER THE CENTURIES, Americans have rarely thought of giving up private property or reducing its importance, but they've eagerly debated what property ownership ought to entail. By the end of the twentieth century, the debate over private property ownership had produced four competing views or interpretations: a libertarian view based on maximum individual autonomy; a more traditional view focused on economic opportunity; a community-centered view in which landownership is an evolving tool to meet community needs; and a biocentric view that looks to the land itself to prescribe the rules for its use. All four interpretations contain nuggets of wisdom, and all four need to be understood to see how land health and measures promoting it can fit together with the institution of private property ownership.

THE LIBERTARIAN IDEAL

Over the course of American history, tensions have always existed between the individual landowner and the surrounding community. On one hand, property ownership reflects values associated with individualism, such as privacy, autonomy, and opportunity; on the other, it reflects values linked to community, such as mutual aid and solidarity. In recent years, individualism has resurged, with vocal defenders of individual liberties attempting to chip away at the community's power. Contemporary champions of the individual have not drawn openly on the Bible, but their rhetoric is recognizable as the Lockean version of paradise regained, with private property ownership as the source of traction.

The centerpiece of this powerful rhetoric is the autonomous human, possessor of essential rights and vigorous participant in the market economy. Had Clayton Williams told his own story, he might have drawn on reasoning such as this, with an emphasis on individuality, freedom, and meaningful boundaries. Wallace Stegner's character Bo Mason might have favored this interpretation, too, for in his quest for riches, he stood alone against the world.

This first perspective on private property ownership, emphasizing individualism, gained considerable ground in the late 1980s. It was spurred on not only by unpopular environmental constraints but also by the publication of a book that presented the view coherently and passionately—*Takings*, by a libertarian law professor, Richard Epstein. Epstein's book leveled a wide-ranging attack on government regulation, particularly land-use rules. It struck a responsive chord and quickly became a leading text not only among libertarian scholars but also among wise-use groups, ardent free-market advocates, and all manner of opponents of environmental rules.

Epstein argued that the rights of a landowner were so fixed and secure that governments could do little to diminish them without paying compensation for any resulting drop in value. The only exception was a law that banned an owner from engaging in land uses so obviously harmful to neighbors as to amount to a physically invasive type of common-law nuisance. As Epstein saw things, a landowner could use his land as he pleased so long as he didn't spew pollution onto neighboring lands or otherwise physically disturb what a neighbor was doing. Laws that went beyond banning such invasive nuisances to restrict other, noninvasive activities interfered with a landowner's vested private rights. Such laws were unconstitutional, and where they were imposed, landowners deserved compensation for resulting losses. Laws that restrained the alteration of wildlife habitat, for instance, were plainly unconstitutional unless compensation was paid. So were laws restricting the draining and filling of wetlands and laws banning construction on ecologically sensitive lands.

Epstein began his book with a story similar to John Locke's. In the early days of pre-history, according to Epstein, humans lived without governments or other communal structures. Land was unowned, and any person could gain ownership of a vacant parcel simply by occupying it. But tensions arose because some people failed to respect the property rights of others, selfishly seizing the fruits of their neighbors' work. Tensions also arose as resources became scarce and people had trouble finding vacant land. In response, people created governments to protect their private rights, vesting them with just enough power to maintain peace. In short, Epstein asserted, ownership of private property came first, and governments were formed to keep it secure.

In his argument, Epstein made extensive use of Locke's writings, particularly Locke's fundamental claim that individual rights existed independently of government and hence trumped the wishes of lawmaking majorities. But where the details of Locke's labor theory didn't really fit his thesis, Epstein quickly revised the theory to meet his needs. The beginning chapter of Locke's story, God's gift of Earth to humans in common, had no place in Epstein's narrative, which was written for a secular audience. Nor did the notion of land initially being owned collectively. If land was owned by everyone, it would be hard to explain how a single individual could seize a parcel and claim ownership without first obtaining group consent. Epstein also rewrote the very centerpiece of Locke's theory—the idea that property rights arose through labor. If working the land translated into ownership, awkward questions quickly arose: How much labor did a person need to expend, and for how long? Could one merely scratch the soil and plant a few seeds, or was major effort required? And what about vacant, undeveloped land? Could a person ever claim ownership of such land, or must it remain unowned until someone finally put it to use? For Locke, the quantity-of-labor issue was a minor detail in his world of presumed abundance, and as for vacant lands, they became government property as soon as governments were created. But all this posed problems for Epstein's argument. In a world of scarcity, the quantity-of-labor question was simply too important to ignore. And if the government took over vacant land, it would presumably possess broad discretion to dictate the terms under which people might use it.

In the face of these challenges, Epstein revised Locke's story materially. Epstein's story begins with unowned land, on which an individual need not labor to gain ownership; he or she merely needed to be the first to occupy it. By eliminating the requirement of labor and allowing a person to gain title to vacant land, Epstein avoided the problems with Locke's argument and denied governments excessive power over unaltered land. Yet as Epstein made these changes to Locke's story, he wiped out all sense that private landownership rewarded a person for labor expended and thus stimulated that labor. He undercut, that is, Locke's primary reason for viewing ownership of private property as a natural right rather than a social creation.

In later writings, Epstein began questioning the entire idea that private property ownership was a natural right, existing independently of any laws or communal approval. First occupancy, Epstein admitted, wasn't the only way for a community to distribute property; it wasn't a natural law of the universe. Nonetheless, it was a simple, low-cost way to allocate resources, as California's gold-rush settlers had realized as they divided the region's rivers and lands. First occupancy, Epstein also recognized, faced objections based on fairness, particularly by those who arrived too late to get in on the original division of things. But that was all right, Epstein decided. Late arrivals were better off anyway, for a world with private property ownership was better than a world without it. Far from complaining about being late, people should be grateful just to live in a world in which ownership of private property was possible.

Epstein plainly was calling for a radical shift in the meaning of private property ownership and in the protection it received under the United States Constitution. He was proposing to his readers, and to the United States Supreme Court, a libertarian alternative to traditional ideas of landownership, an alternative that maximized the freedom of the individual owner to engage in intensive land uses even when these conflicted with the well-being of surrounding communities.

The radical aspects of Epstein's outlook, however, hardly slowed readers who were anxious to embrace his perspective. The chord he struck was among people like Clayton Williams who distrusted government and wanted as little of it as possible. Epstein's audience liked the idea that private landownership created a sphere of influence independent of the state. And they liked the thought that at one time, at least, a person could seize land, develop it, and create value, all without bothering neighbors or seeking permission. Embedded in Epstein's legal argument were elements of the American frontier narrative, a tale of progress and transformation of the land. And at the center of that tale, serving as its protagonist, was the autonomous individual—the Bo Mason of Stegner's novel—disconnected from any community and at liberty to pursue a personally set vision of the good life.

The Traditional Understanding

The second and more truly conservative perspective on private property ownership sinks its roots into traditional understandings of what private property has meant to generations of Americans. It, too, contains an implicit tale of individualism, but its emphasis lies less on autonomy than on self-reliance, mutual respect, and, above all, opportunity. If the neighbor in Frost's poem were to speak out, perhaps he would endorse this traditional understanding. On the contemporary scene, this perspective enjoys support among various members of the United States Supreme Court, most notably Justice Antonin Scalia.

The traditional understanding of property ownership places great weight on property's role in American history, particularly in the late nineteenth century, when the frontier conquest was complete and a market economy dominated. For generations, landless poor from around the world had come to America, gained land, and produced wealth. Along with being a land of opportunity, America was a place of rapid economic growth, and private property ownership was central to that as well. By the end of the nineteenth century, property law had adapted to the new industrial market economy. It had become mature, and in its mature state it protected the individual land parcel as a discrete market commodity and as the indispensable site of domestic life and economic enterprise.

Like Epstein's libertarian view of property ownership, the traditional interpretation sees human labor as adding value to the land. Because landowners can reliably reap where they have sown, owners of private land have an incentive to work hard. As libertarians note, people act industriously only when they stand to gain as individuals, so private landownership must offer them chances to labor and earn wealth. Land development must remain possible, and economic expectations must be protected.

Unlike the libertarian view, however, the traditional interpretation recognizes the reality and utility of human communities. Because land uses are not as discrete as John Locke supposed— their effects spill over property boundaries—the community has the right to regulate an owner's rights and to change them over time, a function largely denied it in the libertarian scheme. But such changes can occur only if property's traditional core functions are adequately preserved.

The traditional understanding of private property ownership— the "historical compact," as Justice Scalia would call it—protects particular core rights, including the right to build a home and otherwise labor on the land in time-honored ways. Landowners have the right to exclude anyone from their property as well as rights to reap, and profit from, the land's produce and to transfer ownership of the land at will. The community has no legitimate interest in what the landowner does within the bounds of his or her own land: A landowner who wants to ruin the soil, strip the trees, or destroy wildlife habitat is free to do so, so long as the harmful effects of such conduct don't traverse the all-important boundary. What the community can rightly control are the adverse effects a landowner has on neighboring land and on the community as a whole—not just physical invasions of neighbors' property, as in the libertarian vision of landownership, but also the effects of land uses that clearly threaten the public's health, safety, or welfare.

This traditional interpretation appeared in several prominent Supreme Court decisions in the late 1980s and early 1990s, most of them written by Justice Scalia. The first prominent case, *Nollan v. California Coastal Commission*, arose in California and involved a landowning couple, the Nollans, who sought a permit to convert their beachfront vacation cottage into a much larger, year-round home. The California Coastal Commission, charged with protecting and enhancing the coastal zone for the common good, was willing to allow the construction but only if the Nollans in return granted the public permission to walk along their beach, up to the high-tide line. As the Supreme Court viewed it, however, this regulatory requirement cut too deeply into the core values of private property ownership, both the right to exclude and the right to build a structure as ordinary as a home. Public access to the beach, the Court agreed, had become difficult. But the Nollans alone hadn't caused the problem, and the state couldn't insist that they and landowners like them solve it. If the public wanted better access, the public should pay for it.

A second Supreme Court decision, *Lucas v. South Carolina Coastal Council*, was also warmly received by conservative audiences. The case involved a land developer, David Lucas, who owned two vacant lots on a barrier island off the coast of South Carolina. Other landowners on the island had built homes, and Lucas merely wanted to do the same. But before he broke ground, the South Carolina legislature, in response to evidence that construction on fragile barrier islands caused many problems, imposed a ban on construction close to the water—a ban that covered David Lucas's lots. As in the Nollans' case, the Supreme Court viewed the state law as the equivalent of a physical taking of Lucas's land. The law, Justice Scalia announced, undercut Lucas's legitimate expectations. As a landowner, he was entitled to make economic use of his land so long as he avoided doing anything traditionally considered harmful, and building a home was almost by definition not harmful. If the state wanted Lucas's land set aside as a nature preserve, it should buy it from him.

As it went about resolving these cases, the Supreme Court appeared troubled by the prospect that a group of lawmakers could simply awaken one day and change all the rules of landownership, with no compensation to those most affected. That power, the Court seemed to say, posed too much of a threat to property's core entitlements. Property ownership couldn't serve its various functions, economic, civic, and personal, unless owners knew they possessed something the state couldn't simply seize, destroy, or redefine out of existence.

The *Lucas* decision drew strong dissent from other members of the Supreme Court who were willing to give South Carolina's legislature greater leeway in balancing environmental goals with the benefits of secure development rights. Over time, the dissenters pointed out, circumstances and values change. Conduct once considered innocuous, even building a house, can come to be viewed as harmful. Ecological effects once ignored or tolerated can become more worrisome. A legislature that had allowed unwise development in the past, before ill effects became known, shouldn't be prevented from changing its course.

As embraced by Justice Scalia, the traditional view of property ownership displays a certain distrust of democracy. Lawmakers can act to halt newly identified harms, but they can't suddenly ban ordinary development even on ecologically sensitive land, at least when landowners have little advance notice. They can't cut too deeply into property ownership's core attributes, and they can do nothing to reduce the landowner's cherished right to exclude.

In 1995, the traditional view of property ownership suffered a modest setback in a Supreme Court case involving the Endangered Species Act, *Babbitt v. Sweet Home Chapter*. Unlike the *Nollan* and *Lucas* cases, *Sweet Home* was not a constitutional challenge; it merely questioned the power of the U.S. Fish and Wildlife Service to restrict private development activity that was likely to kill or injure endangered species. Still, the case cut at the heart of private property ownership—the landowner's right to make economic use of his or her land—and Justice Scalia and the Court's other conservative members disliked the regulations very much. By a narrow margin, the Court upheld the regulations, but it left open the possibility that the regulations might restrict a particular landowner's activities so severely as to amount to an unconstitutional taking of property.

PROPERTY AND THE EVOLVING COMMUNITY

A third understanding of private property ownership focuses on the social community and the ways in which property rules serve the community's evolving needs. Lacking any single author as conspicuous as Richard Epstein or Antonin Scalia, this perspective nonetheless shows up regularly in the discourse and writings of many community advocates, cultural critics, and academics, some concerned with environmental degradation, others with pervasive urban and social ills. One might also attach Aldo Leopold to this perspective, even though his comments on landownership were limited. Leopold didn't speak of the origins of property ownership, but he did perceive it as a cultural creation, arising from people and subject to change by them as their ecological knowledge grew and their moral perspective widened.

The community-centered perspective takes direct issue with John Locke's imagined history of private property's origins. Property really came into existence, advocates of this position note, after, rather than before, human communities arose. Indeed, private property ownership is an institution that makes sense only within a community, among people who have shared interests and who respect one another's entitlements. Far from pre-dating the emergence of states, property is a creation of states; a creation of communities that use it as a means of achieving particular aims, such as maintaining communal solidarity and promoting economic enterprise.

Viewed from this perspective, private property ownership is very much an organic institution, created by people and subject to change by them. Community interests are paramount, and the community can set limits on what landowners do. In the interest of environmental protection, for instance, a community could ban development on ecologically sensitive lands or require landowners to take affirmative steps to promote the welfare of wildlife, or limit harmful drainage practices, or mandate particular types of forestry management.

Proponents of this view warmly embrace the study of history, often noting how landownership rules have varied widely in different times and in different cultures. What they derive from history is not the more tradition-bound bundle of substantive property rights—as in the case of the traditional view of property—but the overriding lessons of continuous change and community control.

Strong individual property rights are not at odds with this view of landownership. A community might decide, for instance, that extensive individual rights usefully promote economic activity and thus indirectly benefit the whole community. But in the end, the benefits that come from secure property rights are subject to conflicting values and trade-offs, and it is up to the community to make those trade-offs—to decide when the individual's wishes will prevail and when the community's will. The only requirement is that a community legislate fairly among landowners with ecologically similar lands and not single out any particular landowner for special burdens.

By granting substantial lawmaking power to the assembled community, this approach to private property ownership rests its faith in the processes of democracy, in the prospect and possibility that over time people will embrace more elevated ethical norms. Advocates of this view often have their own particular ideas about how property law should be shaped, but the ultimate power to make decisions rests with the people. Because the people are in charge, public education becomes an important task. Education is essential, and for advocates working directly with people, so are unending supplies of patience and hope.

The Land As Lawgiver

The fourth view of landownership, based on the land's natural uses, shares features with both the libertarian view and the community-centered view. Like the libertarian alternative, it reflects a great suspicion of democracy and seeks to ground landownership norms in durable values, protected from a misguided populace. Yet it also sees a landscape made up of interdependent pieces, with property rights limited by the community's needs.

In the legal literature, this natural-use narrative found its classic expression in 1972 in a decision of the Supreme Court of Wisconsin. The decision was rendered in the case of *Just v. Marinette County*, involving the validity of a then novel regulation protecting sensitive wetlands. The legal issue before the court was a constitutional one—did the wetland regulation affect the landowner's core property rights to such an extent that the community ought to compensate the landowner for the loss? To get to that constitutional issue, however, the court first had to define ownership, with particular reference to a sensitive parcel such as a wetland.

Early in its opinion, the Wisconsin court framed the relevant question as plainly as it could: "Is the ownership of a parcel of land so absolute," it queried, "that man can change its nature to suit any of his purposes?" To this court, knowing what it did about the ecological roles of wetlands, the answer seemed clear:

> *An owner of land has no absolute and unlimited right to change the essential natural character of his land so as to use it for a purpose for which it was unsuited in its natural state and which injures the rights of others.*

To own sensitive land such as a wetland, the court announced, was to have the right merely to use land in "its natural state" and for its "natural uses"; it didn't include the right to change "the character of the land at the expense of harm to public rights." Nature set its own limits on how land could be used and on the rights landowners could possess.

More than any of the other three views of private property ownership, the natural-use view implicitly embraces the Eden narrative of decline, which portrays the untouched land as a bountiful garden and human-induced change as a cause of degradation. From this perspective, the land itself is the lawgiver, supplier not of the details of ownership but of broad limits beyond which owners may not wander. Landowners may neither materially alter their land nor do anything to disrupt natural ecosystem processes. By vesting such power in the land, this perspective limits considerably the range of private property rights a community can create and thus imposes constraints on democratic processes.

Just v. Marinette County remains a well-loved decision among committed environmentalists, but its pure version of natural property rights has not caught on. Even admirers of the decision realize that nature's ways are not so clear and predictable as to always distinguish good land uses from bad. Ecological processes are complex, and it's often hard to know what effects a land-use change will have on surrounding lands and whether the change will or will not diminish land health. Beyond the nagging difficulties of scientific uncertainty there is discomfort with the idea that people can't make their own laws. To embrace nature itself as a source of rules, binding on lawmakers and without human interpretation, tinkers with much more than the law of private property: It alters the entire idea of sovereignty and public power. The natural-use perspective therefore needs revision to make it tolerable to the modern democratic mind. Nature's integrity can remain a bedrock value and limit, but humans must control the lawmaking process, interpreting the land scientifically and ethically and translating their conclusions and choices into new landownership norms.

Toward a New Narrative of Owning

The environmental movement has stumbled during the past decade in no small part because of clashes over property rights. As many people see it, laws protecting the environment threaten the core values of private property ownership, and the threat seems to be growing. The story of America has been about economic opportunity, landowner independence, and private property ownership—and environmentalism seems to threaten them all; it threatens, that is, the entire progressive narrative that's been so central to America's self-image. The Eden narrative of decline was acceptable so long as it remained a minor, dissenting perspective on the American saga. But as a dominant perspective, it is seen as simply too frustrating and misanthropic.

Despite recent Supreme Court decisions such as *Nollan* and *Lucas*, the Constitution's protection of private property rights imposes only minor restraints on the power of governments to reshape property laws. Legally, states have considerable leeway in drafting land-use rules, banning activities deemed harmful and insisting that landowners fulfill newly imposed obligations. In other words, states have the power to adopt any of the four perspectives on private property and shape their property laws accordingly. Over the long run, their choices will be based on public sentiment along with raw political power, which means that state and local governments will embrace a more ecologically oriented view of property only when the public asks for it or at least stands willing to support it. Public sentiment, of course, is affected by many factors, including awareness of environmental problems and willingness to change behaviors to alleviate them. But to many, property ownership by its very nature is linked with freedom, opportunity, and progress—all at the heart of America's self-identity—and when the law tinkers with ownership rights, it threatens these core values as well.

A central task in the promotion of land health will be the crafting of a new perspective on landownership and, surrounding that, a new perspective on the larger American enterprise. Hardly any conservation task is more important, and work on it has only begun. One environmental narrative of landownership is embedded in the work of the late Edward Abbey, a radical writer whose novels and essays inspired readers to rise up in anger at the land's degradation and to strike back, literally or figuratively, by dumping sugar in the gas tank of the engine of progress. Abbey's narrative has serious flaws and isn't likely to play more than a minor role in the promotion of land health. Yet it is instructive nonetheless and helps illustrate the task that lies ahead.

Abbey lived most of his adult life in the southwestern American desert. He had no thought that humans could improve his chosen home; people only degraded land, just as in the Eden tale of decline. But if Abbey didn't embrace America's vision of endless progress, he latched on as firmly as anyone to its liberal individualism. Like Richard Epstein, Abbey was a libertarian, a firm believer in unyielding individual rights. And like Epstein, he endorsed a view of property ownership in which the landowner's rights were stable and predictable over time. Where he disagreed with Epstein, parting widely from him in fact, was on the core element of individual liberty. For Abbey, liberty meant first and foremost the right to head to the wilds and become part of an unspoiled world, rather than any right to build skyscrapers or golf courses. A country wasn't fit to live in, Abbey proclaimed, "when a man must be afraid to drink freely from his country's rivers and streams." Clean water was as much a civil right as was free speech.

In his peculiar way, Edward Abbey surpassed the zeal of Epstein and other political libertarians. Epstein's fear was of the abuse of power by government; private power, he seemed to say, could be trusted, subject to only minimal restraints on aggression. For Abbey, though, any form of concentrated power was suspect. To his mind, revolution and sabotage were the proper responses to corporate pollution and timber clear-cutting as well as to political oppression. Abbey's radical perspective translated readily into a vision of private landownership. Landowners had secure private rights, to be sure, but they must not pollute the water or air, replace native plants, or drive away resident wildlife. Nature set the baseline for landownership norms, just as it did in the natural-use view of property. Humans were part of the land, just like other animals, but they didn't form harmonious social communities. Attached to the land, they were largely detached from one another.

Abbey stood on the fringe of environmental thought because of his misanthropic views and his emphatic embrace of the Eden tale of decline. He was the frontiersman who set out not to open up wild places so that waves of settlers could follow but to find an isolated spot where he could live unmolested. To enjoy sufficient privacy and to buffer his adverse environmental effects, Abbey's loner needed to own a full square mile of land. In a congested world, Abbey's vision simply wasn't realistic, and in his pragmatic moments Abbey knew it.

Clearly, constructing a new environmental narrative will not be easy. The task is daunting, for a new narrative needs to promote land health and at the same time respect the individual, encourage enterprise, and allow for private rights in land.

For such a story to succeed, it needs to be a tale of progress and hope. Because environmentalists so often oppose development projects and other activities, they commonly assume a negative stance, blocking progress according to their critics, and inhibiting hopes and dreams. Environmentalists are against things, it seems, except for the preservation of lands that people need to leave untouched. In the new century, environmentalism needs to take on a more positive face, casting itself as a movement for the resettlement of America, this time in a mature, durable way. Environmentalism, that is, needs to embrace a narrative of progress in which humans mold the land in healthy ways, meeting their needs through means that are ethically and ecologically sound. In addition, a new environmental narrative needs to emphasize the community much more than the traditional story does, not to the ex-

clusion of the individual but as a vital entity that also deserves respect. Land-use rules should be viewed as expressions of community values and expectations as well as tools the community uses to
promote its goals and defend its well-being. Rules should emerge
from community deliberations and evolve over time as circumstances change and as community members collectively refine
their knowledge and ethical sensibilities.

But if a new environmental narrative is to appeal to modern culture, it also needs to promote private property's privacy and civic
aims, which means respecting the dignity and moral integrity of
the individual landowner. Land-use laws can evolve, yet they need
to change slowly enough that property owners feel sufficiently secure. Ideally, change should occur so smoothly and gradually that
most landowners aren't disrupted by it and don't come to fear it.

Edward Abbey's work suggests another way in which an environmental narrative can respect the individual: by pointing out
how a healthy land expands people's options, protecting them as
individuals from unwanted pollution and degradation. Older liberal ideas offer a similar message: Individuals gain power when
they gather with neighbors in pursuit of collective goals. When a
community has power to act, individuals gain new, collective ways
to achieve their wants. Land-use rules issued by a community may
indeed restrict a landowner's rights, but they also protect landowners, particularly those who depend on clean water, clean air,
and abundant wildlife.

If a more favorable environmental view is to prevail, however,
certain fears must be addressed. One fear, providing fuel for libertarian ideas, is the fear of being excluded from decision-making
processes. Another is the fear that changing laws will disrupt investments, expectations, and opportunities. Laws might become
so unsettled and unpredictable, some think, that investments are
no longer safe. To the excluded outsider, power vested in the community provides a danger, not a new opportunity to achieve collective goals.

The lesson here for environmental policy is plain enough: Ordinary people, particularly landowners, must be drawn into the processes by which land-use decisions are made. Broad-based participation can diminish fears of exclusion. At the same time, it can help landowners become more knowledgeable about environmental problems. And the more knowledgeable people become, the more likely they will be to see land-use restrictions as legitimate responses to real problems rather than the corruption or dismantling of private rights.

In a more progressive environmental tale along these lines, private property ownership can have an honored role, just as it does in Wendell Berry's fiction. Property law can serve as an important, if not indispensable tool for individuals and communities to use as they go about the promotion of land health—listening to the land, tailoring their lives to a place, and settling in for the long term.

Chapter 7

Staying Home

THE BEGINNING POEM in Robert Frost's standard collected works is a short, familiar piece. Titled "The Pasture," it invites the reader to enter Frost's poetry and his special world. "I'm going out to clean the pasture spring;" the poem begins; "I shan't be gone long.—You come too." "I'm going out to fetch the little calf / . . . "I shan't be gone long.—You come too." For half a century and more, Frost plumbed the people and land surrounding his rural Vermont home. In "The Pasture," he encouraged readers to pay him an imaginary visit, to see Vermont through a poet's eyes.

In 1980, Wendell Berry began his volume of poetry *A Part* with a short work titled "Stay Home." It, too, was an invitation, but of a far different kind. "I will wait here in the fields / to see how well the rain / brings on the grass," the poem begins. "I am at home.

Don't come with me. / You stay home too." "In the stillness of the trees / I am at home. Don't come with me. / You stay home too."

"Stay Home," plainly, is a more serious poem than "The Pasture." Where Frost's poem is breezy and lighthearted, "Stay Home" is arresting and peremptory. Berry expects readers to know "The Pasture"; the contrast between the poems is central to his meaning. Like Frost, Berry welcomes vicarious visitors to his world. But unlike Frost, he does so with reservations. Berry is disturbed by armchair naturalists who look fondly at distant places while ignoring the land under their feet. He wants readers to get to know the land around their chosen homes. They should attach themselves, he directs, not to a distant poet's homeland but to their own.

"Stay Home" also contrasts with "The Pasture" in the farm activities the poets undertake. Frost describes quick, active work—fetching the calf and raking leaves away from the pasture spring. The poem catches him as he departs from his house, and he will return there when his chores are done. Berry has quieter business to attend to, closer to nature and more enduring. We find him in his field as the poem opens, and we leave him there at the end. He waits in his field patiently enough to watch the grass grow; standing by the trees, he respects the stillness of the woods. The labor that occurs here, generation on generation, lasts "longer than a man's life." In this labor and this stillness, he is at home and content.

In a few, sure lines, "Stay Home" captures a full set of attitudes and values about land and what it means to stay home. Permanence, rather than transience, is honored; connectedness rather than rootlessness; respect for nature rather than domination. Indeed, the contrast with the noise and anxiety of the modern age could hardly be more stark. Staying home, Berry suggests, is about knowing the land, valuing it, and committing oneself to it.

In his own chosen home, a hillside farm along the Kentucky

River, Wendell Berry uses draft horses rather than tractors because of the farm's slope, small size, and varied terrain. The roughest land remains as a woodlot, which he draws on for timber and firewood as well as mushrooms and nuts. A large garden lies near the river, and various barnyard animals, most raised for home consumption, some raised to trade or sell, inhabit adjacent pens and pastures. Aside from a few head of cattle, Berry's main cash crop is sheep, which he breeds in the hope of developing a strain perfectly suited to hilly, marginal lands like his own: animals agile enough to manage living on this kind of land, able to flourish on native grasses, and capable of dropping lambs with little or no human help. A few level acres are devoted to row crops, but most of the farm is divided into pastures, with animals moved regularly to avoid overgrazing and erosion. Every year, he tinkers with the mix of land uses, constantly trying to get the proportions right.

Berry writes often about this place and the thinking that motivates and guides his farming methods. He writes with clarity and passion, yet he is sometimes misunderstood. Hearing of his draft horses, readers consider him a Luddite, his nostalgic ideas irrelevant to the high-volume, high-technology operations that dominate modern farming. What readers grasp only slowly is that Berry isn't encouraging them to mimic his ways. He farms the way he does because his land is what it is; poor land, long abused, and not suitable for modern equipment. He raises sheep because cattle are too destructive for his slopes and can't maneuver well on them. Berry's message for his readers is more general and distilled: that they, like he, should tailor their lives to what nature offers. Before using land, they should ask what nature is doing there and how they might use the land consistently with its long-term fertility. To stay home is to become attentive to a chosen place and let nature shape the methods and rhythms of everyday life.

IMAGINING THE LAND

For Berry, staying home responsibly requires a great deal of work and a sure moral compass. It's not the easy job—the lazy, ambitionless option—that the modern mind so often supposes. Staying home requires engaging with one's surroundings, natural and human, and forging respectful ties with them. Over time, an affectionate familiarity can arise between person and place as the land community becomes an extension of the mind and heart of the resident. Staying home also requires an understanding of the land's past. Where memories are weak or absent, a land steward needs to seek out local people who do remember, examine local records, and study the land itself for evidence of what it once was and how it's been used.

A central part of staying home is giving thought to the future and considering those who will eventually inherit the land. Future generations are prepared for by tending the land well and by asking questions about its prospects and possibilities: How might the land change after decades or generations of good tending? What could it yield, and at what levels, if it were truly healthy? To answer such questions, an owner begins, as Wendell Berry did, by looking to the land's history.

When Berry first came to his farm, he knew that its past differed greatly from its present. The land had possessed a deep reservoir of topsoil when white settlers arrived on the scene. The trees were larger and taller and native species more diverse. Arriving settlers had cut the trees to open the land for farming and human occupation. That work, transforming the wild into a pastoral landscape, was necessary and good; without it, only dispersed hunter-gatherers could have occupied the land. But Kentucky's early settlers failed to care for the land well. In their quest to grow crops, they tilled lands that should have gone unbroken. They introduced animals that weren't suited to the land. Acting in haste, they ignored the land's integrity.

When Berry thinks about the future of his farm and the surrounding lands, he is mindful of this history of inattention and misuse. Once, neighborhood dwellers could shape a decent life around fishing, hunting, trapping, and gathering, given the land's diversity and the abundance of river life. The forage production of fields was greater due to the soil's depth and fertility. Woodlots produced better timber because good trees remained. Thoughts of these early times move Berry greatly as he considers the land's future and the work that has fallen to his generation. With enough time and good work, he believes, the land's fertility, diversity, and beauty could all return, given nature's forgiving temperament. And so, perhaps, might the vibrant small towns and rural culture Berry knew as a youth, although the odds here are long, given the potent economic forces that have depopulated the countryside and driven shoppers to distant malls and discount stores.

Yet as much as Berry reveres the past, he isn't out to revive it completely. For him, pristine natural areas don't supply the model of ideal land, though he uses them for guidance and inspiration. People have a legitimate role on the land, working with it, changing it with their labor, and increasing its yield. But to fulfill that role well, a person must undertake the hard work of staying home, recognizing nature's constraints and peculiarities and living at peace within them.

The modern environmental movement says little about the task of staying home and has done little to encourage people to imagine how the lands around them might improve, ecologically and aesthetically. To be sure, campaigns to restore wetlands and riparian corridors do aim to improve the land, as do proposals to recover native biodiversity. Similarly, efforts to reform the USDA Forest Service are guided by hopes that in time, public forests will recover from the clear-cuts and monocultures that have reduced some complex forest ecosystems to mere tree farms. But most environmental programs don't call on people in ordinary places to look closely at the land around them.

For land health to return to the back hills of Kentucky, the little-noted rivers of Illinois, and the distant ranchlands of Wyoming, local residents need to exercise their imagination and consider how their environs might improve under decades of good care. Plainly, local water and air might be cleaner and river corridors and hydrologic cycles more natural, with fewer human-aided floods and droughts. But as imaginations are spurred and deliberations continue, communal efforts should move toward a broader vision of land health. Wildlife communities might become more diverse and balanced, with many native species restored to their original ranges and with reduced populations of opportunistic, aggressive species that thrive on human-caused disruption. Farm fields and timber lots might appear less regimented and artificial, with landowners shifting to methods that feature greater species diversity, generate fertility within each field, and slowly add to the indispensable fund of soil. Patches of wild might exist beside patches of intensive use, with big nature preserves set aside to sustain species that need undisturbed habitat and with deliberate steps taken to restore disrupted ecosystem processes such as prairie fires. Communities might increase their consumption of locally produced food, with citizens knowing where, how, and by whom their food is produced. Local lands, as they increase in diversity and beauty, might provide more appealing recreational opportunities, encouraging people to stay closer to home and spend their dollars there.

Thinking Locally

In 1972, philosopher and scientist René Dubos coined the slogan "Think globally, act locally," and the environmental movement quickly embraced it. The sentiment was useful and well-intentioned, encouraging people to work locally while recognizing how local behavior affects the larger scene. But the slogan overlooked the dangers associated with global thinking. To the globally focused mind, problems exist on a grand scale, demanding equally grand solutions. Technology and ideas are shifted from one place to another with little regard for local circumstances, and local problems and possibilities become easy to miss. Global thinking can also breed a sense of helplessness. If a problem is global in scope, how can the work of local people possibly make a dent in it?

Along Boneyard Creek in Champaign-Urbana, Illinois, global thinking is very much evident. Local residents aren't indifferent to beautiful, flowing rivers, but many display the same national or global attitude toward nature as they do toward the economy. The rivers worth caring for are in those in Idaho, Colorado, or Minnesota, not ordinary prairie streams such as the Boneyard. Possessed of a global focus, local residents think more about destruction in the Amazon basin than about degradation of a modest neighborhood river. Looking at the horizon, they overlook what is at their feet. Scanning a thousand rivers quickly, they study no place with attention and care.

Too readily, a globally turned mind can develop a sense of disdain for the local, undervaluing it and missing its complexities and possibilities. Cascading, picture-postcard waterways in distant places seem more worth visiting and protecting; next to them, even the most attractive prairie creek simply doesn't measure up. The same attitude affects species preservation, with local species often ignored in favor of grizzly bears, whales, and whooping cranes in distant places. Redwood forests demand attention because they're national or international assets; local oak-hickory forests can fend for themselves.

Such a regionally dismissive attitude spills over into other aspects of people's lives, disconnecting them from their place in the ecosystem. Few citizens, for example, know where their drinking water comes from, particularly in urban areas. Even fewer know where their wastes go when the garbage truck drives away. For most consumers, produce in the food market merely appears on the shelves, its history unknown except when advertisers see gains in telling people that apples have journeyed from Washington or potatoes from Idaho. Goods come from the vast global market; they come from everywhere, which is to say from nowhere.

Like people elsewhere, residents along the Boneyard eat food that is largely produced far away and that is often grown, raised, or processed in ways that cause harm. Energy also comes from a distance and is generated in ways that create problems, whether in the mine fields of Kentucky or in Prince William Sound. Outgoing wastes are shipped not just out of the watershed but out of the county, to someone else's backyard. Distant places such as these, where goods come from and where wastes go, form the backstage areas of people's lives, the places that people don't see yet that are so much a part of human ecology. Particularly to a mind focused globally, backstage areas are easily overlooked in the bustle of daily living. It's easy to forget about the distant strip mines, the eroding farm fields, the pesticide-laced aquifers, the hazardous waste drums, and the utility smokestacks—all operating to meet local demands. When environmental degradation occurs locally, a globally minded person tends to dismiss the harm; when the degradation occurs elsewhere, the same mentality can encourage a person to discount his or her own, seemingly trivial contributing role.

If René Dubos were alive today, perhaps he would reconsider his slogan and downplay the benefits of global thinking. In any event, it is increasingly apparent that a new, more local way of thinking is needed, a way of thinking that encourages people to know the specific ways in which they're connected to the natural world. A person firmly attached to a particular place is likely to have strong protective feelings about that place. Knowing the dangers confronting one's home, it becomes easier to realize that other places, too, are at risk, places that also have people affectionately attached to them. To buy food that comes from a distant place is to take food from someone else's homeland and hence to become involved in that person's life.

Good local thinking, then, recognizes that connectedness to

the land is universal, that distant people are as connected to their homes as are nearby people. A person who knows the history of locally produced goods—who knows, that is, how and where local products were raised or made and the consequences of their production—is likely to realize that all goods have such histories. Food never appears spontaneously at the grocery store. Once this connection is made, a consumer might alter his or her purchasing decisions—perhaps opting for organic vegetables over pesticide-treated produce in order to reduce the hazards of pesticide exposure to farmworkers, perhaps choosing produce sold at a farmers' market in order to support local farms.

Such thinking stands in stark opposition to the dogma embraced by many free-market thinkers, who view the market as an agent that strips goods of their histories and hence frees purchasers from any responsibility for those histories. In free-market theory, buyers of goods have legitimate interests only in the quality of the goods themselves, not in how or where they were produced and what harm may have come from their production. Goods are fungible items, freely traded in the market.

Regrettably, this type of thought also appears in international trade laws, which commonly allow countries to exclude foreign goods only if they're unsafe or unhealthy. In a notorious case, the United States was found to have engaged in unfair trade practices when it kept Mexican tuna out of the country, not because the tuna was somehow unhealthy but because the fish were caught in nets that needlessly killed dolphins. According to the international court, the United States as a national community had no connection to, and thus no right to worry about, the needless dolphin killing that accompanied the tuna harvest.

A decision such as this, stripping away a product's damaging past, makes little sense. A person who buys a product is implicated in its history, just as a person who generates waste is morally involved in its disposal.

The Local Community

Staying home responsibly requires more of a person than just sound living as an individual. He or she must belong to the local community and participate openly in it. Interactions with one's neighbors need to include emotive elements and patterns of sharing. Such interactions, giving rise to a sense of belonging and wholeness, are vital to softening boundaries and promoting connections.

Today, community participation is based mostly on occupational group, avocational interest, former school affiliation, and the like—on factors, that is, other than living in the same place at the same time. But it is a grave mistake to discount territory-based senses of community, particularly in rural areas. Aside from their social benefits, place-based communities recognize that people sharing a landscape are joined by nature and thus necessarily intermingle their fates. Never does a ravaging drought affect a single family's land; climatic disturbances affect everyone, and people afflicted in similar ways tend to turn to one another for help. The verb "to neighbor" is alive and well in rural communities across America, as it is to varying degrees elsewhere though links and interdependencies may be harder to see.

Place-based communities also give landowners a sense that their work is part of a larger enterprise, more encompassing and durable than any single person or generation. Families committed to a single farm for generations often have this sense; they recognize the land's longevity and see their farm as an intergenerational asset. But farmers need to go beyond this sense of attachment to see themselves also as stewards of the greater landscape, given the inevitable interconnectedness of land uses. Owners need to grasp how their lands fit with surrounding lands to form a natural whole, just as their own generation joins with others to form an enduring human settlement.

A local community can play a further important role as an information clearinghouse for land-use ideas so that a community member grappling, for instance, with a drainage concern or a pest outbreak can readily consult with others who've faced similar challenges. Without local exchanges, landowners often must rely on information provided by corporations, which are chiefly out to sell products, or from the government. Information obtained through government channels is commonly less biased, but it, too, comes from people whose aims overlap only partially with those of local landowners—people with careers to advance, research grants to gain, and agency budgets to pad. And even government-provided information is influenced by industry groups, which shape and finance both government and academic research agendas. In contrast, local people tend to be concerned about one another and the community as such. When information sharing like this occurs, it strengthens communities and fosters a sense of bondedness at the same time that it generates a fund of helpful, locally tailored knowledge.

Another vital function of the community stems from its inevitable role in setting informal standards of behavior. Whether strict or relaxed, informal standards have potent effects on community residents, helping shape how they see themselves, what they value, and how they judge right and wrong. If local people see beauty in a soybean field that's free of weeds, farmers will probably till the soil and spray the crop with herbicides; conversely, if local people perceive harm in unnecessary tillage and spraying and prefer a more natural land aesthetic, many farmers will adapt their practices accordingly. When front yards in a suburb are manicured and weed-free, pressure is placed on homeowners to conform, even though some might prefer more natural lawns.

Community-set standards can assume many forms, and good ones can greatly aid the quest for land health, reducing the need for more formal, legal controls. For example, if enough people in a community come to see beauty in native plants and in diverse polycultures, such plantings might soon prevail. If conservation-tillage practices become the norm for sound farming and beautiful fields, the farmer who plows every season will feel pressure to change. Although norms such as these can be hard to establish, their potential power is considerable, as the development of antismoking norms illustrates. Household recycling, another good norm, has become an accepted behavior pattern in many places, as entrenched as standards against littering. Among hunters, wasteful or unsportsmanlike killing is roundly scorned. Hope exists, therefore, that community standards might evoke greater ecological sensitivity in such activities as timber harvesting, lawn care, drainage, waste disposal, landscaping, pesticide use, grazing, wildlife habitat, and river-corridor management.

In sum, place-based communities can play a vital role in the promotion of land health by broadening people's sense of belonging, stimulating local knowledge, and fostering sensible behavior standards. But communities of this type will succeed only if they are valued and actively promoted by their residents, who need to recognize that their personal interests blend with those of the community. The blending, of course, is only partial—the individual still counts and has separate aims—but the community also must count. Such blurring of lines occurs instinctively in many families. The individual is important, but so is the family. Like it or not, membership in such a family partially defines who a person is individually. In similar ways, a good community member respects group norms and helps promote the group's good. The blending, again, is far from complete. But the individual helps compose the whole and in turn is partially defined by it.

In Wendell Berry's fictional Port William, Mat Feltner is woven tightly in conduct and values into the fabric of his hometown. He realizes that he belongs to something bigger than his land and his family, and he devotes time and energy to that larger being. By proving himself worthy, Mat has become a community leader and instinctively steps forward to do his share. He is the kind of person who would naturally help his community respond to landscape-scale environmental problems. Placed in today's context, perhaps he would advocate cooperative marketing or help organize a community-supported agriculture project for the mutual benefit of farmers and urban food buyers. Perhaps he would take up the idea of watershed planning, encouraging neighbors to join him in studying regional problems and searching for fair, cooperative ways to deal with them.

But as Mat Feltner reached beyond his immediate neighbors and friends, he'd inevitably encounter resistance; Berry is too honest a novelist to have it otherwise. Throughout rural areas, liberal individualism is strongly entrenched, particularly in its conservative forms, and so is free-market thought. Private property is respected, and land use is deemed a private matter so long as neighbors aren't overtly harmed.

One of Mat's prime challenges as community leader would be to soften these attitudes. He'd need to get other landowners to see that land use isn't just a private matter but has serious public repercussions. In Mat's own case, owning has a lot to do with belonging, and to belong is to recognize that one is a part of something larger. Like Berry himself, Mat lacks the individualistic, commodity-oriented mentality of the modern age. As he surveys his farm boundary, he's fully aware of its permeability and so feels linked to everything around him. Loving his land as he does and respecting his community, he shoulders his duties willingly and encourages others to follow his lead.

Mat Feltner's community, apparently, is blessed with enough good land stewards and has sound enough standards of expected conduct that it needs no formal land-use controls. Landowners need not be coerced to act responsibly. But Port William is an anomaly. Mat's challenges in dealing with ecological problems would increase as he reached beyond his neighborhood to landowners elsewhere, many of them firmly oriented toward the market and strong private property rights. Mat's hope, no doubt, would be that these landowners might respond to moral suasion, volun-

tarily becoming more like him and like those whom he's long admired, the people who've loved the land and embraced its interconnections, who've shown concern for future generations and
taken pleasure in gazing on bountiful land. Given a choice, that is,
Mat would rely on education, discussion, and social pressure rather
than coercive legal measures. But he would soon recognize, if he
didn't know it already, that not all local residents are willing to acknowledge problems and respond voluntarily. And Mat would also
recognize, if he didn't know it simply by gazing at the polluted
Kentucky River, that his local community is at the mercy of powerful outside forces, such as the miners upstream whose refuse
loads the river.

COMMUNITY POWER

For a quarter century, promotion of community action has been
the primary aim of the Central States Education Center, an
Illinois-based environmental organization that helps citizens deal
with environmental problems. Over the years, the Center has
worked with groups opposed to specific reservoirs and landfills.
Recently, it has begun promoting citizen interest in restoration
and preservation of Illinois rivers. Around the state, groups have
formed to deal with waterway problems, some flood related, others caused by rapid development, still others caused by pollution
and general river-corridor deterioration. The Center wants more
such groups to form, and has formed a network to transmit good
ideas from place to place.

In talking with representatives of groups around the state, the
Center's director, Rob Moore, hears particular complaints again
and again. Rural landowners are suspicious of collective action,
particularly any action that might threaten their property rights or
curtail their activities. In addition, many landowners refuse to see
problems or, if they see them, are unwilling to trace them back to
drainage lines, erosive land-use patterns, or other underlying

causes. Finally, many landowners are burdened by a sense of help-lessness. They wish their local river were cleaner and more nat-ural, and they're willing to help improve it. But as individuals, they feel helpless. River problems arise from the decisions of dozens, hundreds, or even thousands of landowners, and good conduct by any one of them seemingly makes no difference.

As Moore sees matters, a key problem in river issues is that rel-evant land-use decisions aren't made at the community level: They're made at the individual level, by landowners and develop-ers pursuing their own narrow interests. In the case of rivers hard-pressed by development, for instance, the very same people who endorse protection are sometimes among the first to rush in to cut trees and build riverfront houses. Their conduct appears anom-alous, but it is less so than it first seems. The person who favors preservation may be willing to forgo joining in on a development rush, but only if others forgo as well. If the land is going to be de-veloped anyway, why stand back while others enjoy the benefits? Few people want to make sacrifices and change their ways only to find that as they refrain from destructive acts, other people take their place. If a wooded river corridor is going to turn into a resi-dential development, why hang back and let others buy the nice homes?

At work here is a force referred to as the tyranny of small deci-sions. When people make decisions in isolation, acting solely as in-dividuals, they often act in ways far different from what they'd choose if asked as citizens to identify the common good. As a con-sumer, a person might buy a new house along the river; as a citizen, the same person might vote to impose development restrictions. One difference, as critics of communal action point out, is that cit-izens can be more willing to protect resources when someone else pays the costs. But a more substantial difference is that people make choices according to their knowledge of problems and the amount of time they've spent reflecting on them. Decisions made by citi-zens in concert tend to be more ethical and more responsive to long-term concerns. When deliberative processes work well, participants often recognize their communal ties and shared interests, embracing more ecological perspectives and thinking of themselves less as isolated individuals.

Yet another reason why citizen choices often differ from consumer preferences is that communities have powers far beyond those of individuals. River protection requires concerted action; no individual, however ardent his or her riparian desire, can choose the protection option. For the individual, the choice is sometimes disturbingly simple: Either participate in the river's degradation or stand back and let others do it.

What Rob Moore knows from experience is that communities must act collectively if ecological problems are to subside, and collective action often must take the form of mandatory measures such as land-use regulations. For collective action to happen, however, local people need to have more faith in their government. Too often, government is viewed as an enemy or as a force dominated by special interests. This hostility toward government must be overcome. Suspicions are exacerbated when land-use rules emanate from distant governments, far from the local scene, and residents rightfully wonder whether local conditions and options have been duly weighed in their formulation. Yet negative reactions to land-use rules also arise because people respond to them in their capacities as individuals and consumers, not taking the time as citizens to appreciate the problems at stake and to see the reasonableness of options selected. Making matters worse is the potent spirit of competition within and between communities. Producers have competed with one another for so long, so intensely, and with so many losers that the fabric of cooperation has been weakened and frayed.

If land health is to come about, communities need to regain lost ground and citizens need to view their government in more positive ways, as the orderly means by which communities can achieve shared goals. For this to happen, people need to become more involved at the local level in deliberative processes that stimulate good study, discussion, and planning. Discussions need to range widely, covering such matters as ethics and aesthetics as well as the immediate challenges of the day. And as people talk and reflect, they need to act more as citizens and less as independent consumers and producers. From these interactions and reflections can come a far clearer sense not just of land health but also of community well-being and the meaning of responsible citizenship: a sense of what it means to stay home.

Chapter 8

Gaining Wisdom
from the Prairie

ONE OF THE MOST deliberate efforts to tailor human life to a place is unfolding in the former tallgrass prairie outside Salina, Kansas, at an unusual research center and school called the Land Institute. There, Dr. Wes Jackson and a team of researchers are working to develop more ecologically sound methods of agriculture. Modern farming methods, they believe, are ultimately destructive and unsustainable: regular plowing erodes soil on flat lands as well as sloping ones; chemical pesticides and fertilizers gradually degrade soil quality; and heavy farm equipment gulps fossil fuels, pollutes air, and compacts the ground. As Jackson sees it, these problems are solvable only by radically changing the ways people get sustenance from the ground. A new approach is needed, and the Land Institute is trying to develop it.

Farming Nature's Way

The work of the Land Institute is unusual not only in its ambitious goals but also in its humble approach to the land. The Institute's guiding premise is that nature has evolved ways of overcoming the very problems that beset modern agriculture. Whereas annual monocultures cause loss of soil, sometimes at precipitous rates, native plant communities have evolved ways of retaining and building it. Unlike modern farmlands, native plant communities also excel at retaining rainfall and maximizing moisture use, and as they do so, they moderate water flows, diminishing the likelihood of both flood and drought. Whereas farm crops typically need imported fertilizers, native communities include nitrogen-fixing species, which help sustain nearby nitrogen users. And native communities, having evolved strategies to counter insects and other pests, have no need for the artificial pesticides that bathe most farm monocultures.

The specific farm setting where Wes Jackson and his colleagues work provides a perfect laboratory for testing new farming methods. On one side of the Institute lies a never-plowed tallgrass prairie, the native plant community. Fire disturbs it and droughts come and go, yet the prairie remains vigorous. Institute staff study the prairie constantly, trying to tease out the reasons for its success. On the other side lie commercial wheat fields, which are plowed annually and planted with a single species. Each plant is genetically identical to the next and hence has the same nutrient and moisture needs and the same susceptibility to pests. Freshly plowed and newly planted fields are highly vulnerable to erosion, and even when the wheat is mature, the soil-retaining root mass below-ground is relatively modest.

The contrast between these wheat fields and the native prairie is stark. The prairie features perennial plants, not annual ones, whose roots grip the soil year-round. More than two hundred species are native to the prairie, and many of them show wide genetic variation. Some species do particularly well in dry years; in wet years, other plants thrive. When pests attack particular prairie species, other species are usually untouched, and pests multiply more slowly than in the wheat field because their target plants are widely spread. Symbiotic relationships occur among prairie species, with some providing nitrogen that others use and some thwarting pests with natural, built-in insecticides; still others provide shade, foster moisture retention or supply various other ecological benefits. Overall, the prairie's success is due in large part to cooperative relationships and community context. The whole is greater than the sum of its parts, which means the prairie can't be fully understood by studying each part in isolation.

The Land Institute's goal is to construct what Wes Jackson calls a domestic prairie—that is, a model ecosystem for grain production that is specifically suited to the soils, terrain, and climate of places such as Salina, Kansas. Like the native prairie, such a system would feature a polyculture of perennial species, derived from the native prairie yet bred to increase seed yield and resistance to seed shatter and pests. Although there would be much less species diversity than in the native prairie—perhaps constituting only a handful of different species—the mix of plants would nonetheless include nitrogen fixers in order to eliminate the need for chemical fertilizers. In the end, researchers hope, the domestic prairie will take on the beneficial characteristics of the native prairie but with a vastly enhanced ability to produce grains for human consumption.

The Institute has set a daunting task for itself, for the prairie doesn't yield its secrets easily. Researchers don't expect ever to understand the ecosystem fully. But they still believe they can take advantage of nature's built-in wisdom even when it isn't fully understood. Scientists imitating nature don't have to understand fully the why and the how to enjoy success.

Besides pointing out the values of ecological agriculture, the work at the Land Institute illustrates the advantages of staying home. The thinking here is decidedly local, focusing on local needs and local opportunities. In the view of Wes Jackson, a native Kansan, solutions to environmental problems are largely at hand, in the adjacent prairie and in the skills of local people. The key is to find them and put them to use.

Among the local solutions being sought are on-farm ways of generating energy so that a farm in central Kansas doesn't depend on the flow of fossil fuels from areas far away. At the Sunshine Farm, an allied research center down the road from the Institute, researchers are studying farm energy-use patterns and investigating alternative energy sources. Native sunflowers are grown and pressed to produce vegetable oil, which is then used to power tractors and other equipment. The ramifications of this research, if successful, are profound.

Overall, the Institute's orientation to the land has a distinct spiritual element, despite its rigorous and innovative science. Staff members possess a reverence for the land and a respect for the forces that produced it. The native prairie, they realize, is no Garden of Eden, at least not for humans: Few prairie plants produce much food that people can eat, and the overall seed yield is low. Still, there is a strong sense that the native species are desirable and beautiful as well as loaded with practical wisdom. Ultimately, they believe, the best way to worship nature is by imitation.

IMITATING NATURE

As a way of relating to the land, the imitation of nature is gradually winning converts, and its potential applications are many. In the American West, grazing regimes that imitate nature's approach—as practiced by wide-ranging herds of bison—are proving far less damaging to natural plant communities, soils, and waterways than the artificial cattle-grazing practices ranchers commonly employ. Similarly, mixed-age, mixed-species forests sustain the soil much better and provide richer wildlife habitat than do the tree farms many timber companies operate. Roads that follow natural contour lines have fewer drainage problems. Waterways that meander naturally sustain aquatic life better, have higher water quality, and suffer less from stream-bank erosion than do straight-line ditches.

Aside from these resource-management issues, nature offers guidance in other settings as well. Many animals wisely use the land itself to protect themselves from temperature extremes; human building designs can do the same, taking advantage of earth sheltering to provide protection from cold and heat. Grazing and browsing animals keep the land's fertility cycles intact by returning their wastes to the very soil that nourishes their food; again, people could take lessons from nature's simple yet elegant ways of keeping soil fertile.

To take advantage of nature's built-in wisdom—to use nature as the measure—humans need not attempt to duplicate exactly the native ecosystems (such as the tallgrass prairie) that are being used as models. They need not, for instance, try to reintroduce every species that is native to a place in the way a restoration ecologist might. Still, nature does impose a severe discipline on researchers; people are by no means free to reshape plant communities at will. They need to act cautiously and humbly, recognizing that nature's hidden mysteries are many and that deference is in order. Many species, for instance, play important community roles that we understand vaguely if at all, and the community would function less well without them. Of course, even aside from the functional roles particular species play, people could choose to protect or reintroduce them for other vital reasons, based on aesthetics or ethics.

When researchers at the Land Institute turn to the prairie, they look for fundamental principles and interactions, not exact mixes and populations of species. As they do this, they constantly ask questions, look for answers, and then form new questions. Theirs is a trial-and-error method often referred to as adaptive land management. Rather than dictating to the land as do nearby wheat farmers, they converse with it, treating it as a coequal subject rather than a mere object. To live on the land in this way, using it and learning from it, is to engage in a type of conversation. Gradually, as Wendell Berry has put it, the conversation can take on "a kind of creaturely life, binding the place and its inhabitants together, changing and growing to no end, no final accomplishment, that can be conceived or foreseen."

Dealing with the land in this manner is not a new idea. Indeed, the imitation of nature has deep roots in human culture. It draws on the tradition of mimesis, the process of imitation, which features a more experiential, intuitive approach toward the land. In this tradition, people participate in the life of the land and are less detached from it. They see the land from the perspective of an insider; the land is a community, and they are members of it.

OWNERSHIP NORMS

All human interactions with nature would benefit from the dedicated, respectful localism that drives the work of Wes Jackson and his colleagues. In terms of cultural institutions, perhaps none would benefit more than the body of laws and legal processes that set forth the rules by which people use nature. Property law, broadly conceived to include natural resources law, could improve greatly if it paid more attention to the land and didn't focus so exclusively on the competing interests of people. Guided by nature, property law could reflect greater ecological awareness while promoting a more aesthetically pleasing landscape in line with evolving ethical values. Well-crafted landownership laws can express a community's growing understanding of nature and its willingness to respect nature's limits. Moreover, as a tool, property law provides a way for a community to deal with recalcitrant landowners inclined to continue old patterns of abuse, to the detriment of neighbors and the community at large.

One way property law can be guided by nature is by tailoring a landowner's rights to the land itself, allowing the owner of a particular tract to engage only in those land uses that are consistent with the health of the larger natural community. A wetland isn't the same as a dry field in ecological terms, and property law shouldn't treat the two land types alike. Similarly, a sloping hillside isn't the same as a flat field; hillside owners might appropriately be limited to those activities that maintain the soil and limit runoff. Land that sits atop the recharge area of a drinking-water aquifer should carry different ownership rights from land grounded on bedrock. When property law takes such differences into account and shapes land-owner rights around them, it displays a more humble attitude, a willingness to bend to nature rather than to dominate it.

Property law can also broaden the range of activities considered harmful to include actions that disrupt vital ecosystem processes. In the past, property law typically recognized harm only when a landowner's activities disturbed neighbors in an obvious and immediate way. Today, science has made clear that a wide range of human activities harm the land, sometimes in ways that are invisible, slow, and indirect. Unnecessary harm occurs, for example, when a farmer drains a river to grow crops that could be produced elsewhere with no ill effects. Single-species tree farms that adversely affect wildlife, exacerbate soil erosion, and require regular chemical applications could also be considered harmful. And a community could perceive harm when a riverfront home builder cuts trees along a river, degrading the riparian corridor just so home buyers can have picturesque views.

As a community becomes more ecologically sophisticated, its property laws are likely to move beyond cases such as these, involving specific land uses with rather obvious damaging effects, to deal with land uses that are innocent enough in isolation but cause harm when too many people engage in them. Many actions are tolerable or even desirable when a few people engage in them but when too many people do so, they can push a landscape beyond its carrying capacity. Drainage lines, which may be harmless as stand-alone structures, can lead to massive flooding when enough people employ them. Small amounts of pollution in a waterway may have little effect on aquatic life; enough of it, though, and populations can plummet. Similarly, destruction of wildlife habitat can reach a point at which native biodiversity becomes seriously disturbed and particular species reach the brink of extinction.

Harms such as these, ones that relate to the land's carrying capacity, are hard to deal with in ways landowners consider fair, yet land health will remain elusive until they're redressed. In the past, when communities have tried to deal with limits to carrying capacity, they've typically waited until the land's limit was reached and then drawn a line, prohibiting any more landowners from engaging in the same land use or activity. Those landowners already engaging in the use or activity are allowed to keep doing what they're doing; all others are subjected to the new legal ban. Many people view such laws as grossly unfair or discriminatory, since they favor some landowners over others, even where lands are ecologically similar. Indeed, so adamant are such claims of unfairness that many communities are loath to reform their property laws; immobilized by criticism, they let land quality degrade.

Fortunately, various legal techniques exist to deal with the fairness issue, but they are available only if a community looks ahead and puts new rules in place before the land is pushed to the brink. One promising technique involves the use of transferable development rights, or TDRs. When a community wants only limited development in a particular area, such as a sensitive wildlife habitat, an erodible hillside, or an aquifer recharge area, it can set an overall development limit in advance. That limit can be phrased in any of a number of ways—in terms of number of structures permitted, amount of drainage or vegetation removal that can occur, or extent of allowable paving or terrain modification, for example. Once the limit is in place, the law can divide the overall development load into individual shares and allocate those shares fairly among all landowners, typically in proportion to the size of their lands in the area. Landowners who choose not to develop can sell their development rights to other landowners in the same area; those who want to develop more than their share can buy rights from others. In this manner all landowners participate in the economic benefits of development, and all are curtailed by development limits. Landowners are dealt with fairly and the land's overall limits are respected.

The old way of dealing with limits to carrying-capacity amounted to a first-in-time method of allocating development rights, the same method California courts used to resolve water disputes in the gold-rush days. As an allocation scheme, the first-in-time system isn't the most unfair method—it's far better, of course, than corrupt methods of political favoritism or bribery—but communities have trouble drawing lines and sticking with them. When a limit is imposed, the people next in line to develop can form a powerful interest group pressing for more relaxed land-use rules. And in contemporary politics, small interest groups with much to gain by legal action quite often get their way.

In the case of California's rivers, nature itself drew the line: When a river ran dry, later arriving settlers got no water. But land health starts declining long before rivers are drained dry, just as wildlife communities are harmed long before the last habitat is destroyed and just as rivers are damaged by harmful drainage practices well before floods become devastating. Communities that are mature in their ecological and ethical awareness will want to protect themselves from more subtle harms. Indeed, they'll probably want to err on the side of safety, setting limits on development clearly below the level at which discernible harm is predicted to become excessive.

To draw lines like that, respecting nature's limits and providing an ample margin of safety, is a hard job, particularly in places with strong development pressure. By addressing the fairness issue, TDR schemes can make that job a bit easier. But even with the fairness issue reduced, line drawing requires courage, along with a clear sense of land health. Community leaders aren't likely to have that courage unless the community itself stands behind them, understanding what they are doing and why. For its part, the community needs to have a clear sense of the kind of landscape it wants, and it needs to defend that landscape from the powerful economic forces pushing against it.

As a community crafts new laws to deal with carrying capacity issues and otherwise goes about broadening its sense of land-use harm—in all cases using nature as its measure—it needs to pay particular attention to the conservation of those natural resources that are vital to sustained life, particularly the soil itself. In the libertarian and traditional views of private property ownership, landowners have the right to destroy what they own so long as their destructive acts don't bother other landowners. Thus, a timber company can manage hillside trees in such a way that the land becomes barren in a century if that's the way it wants to exercise its rights. Ranchers can graze their lands so that palatable native plants disappear and cheat grass and thistles take over. Miners can strip the land surface to get at underlying coal and then walk away from the ruins.

Conduct like this degrades the common landscape, even when confined within the boundaries of private parcels, and the entire land community suffers from it. In an ownership scheme more sensitive and respectful of the land, landowners would have no right to do these things. To own land would entail an obligation to care for it sufficiently well that it remained valuable for later users. Ownership would not include the right to destroy.

Fairness and the Taking of Private Land

The work of tailoring property rights to the land, drawing on nature's embedded wisdom, will not prove easy. The challenges will be many, and high on the list is the inevitable claim that changes in property rights unfairly disrupt landowner expectations. Indeed, this complaint has already become common, as illustrated notably by the case of David Lucas of South Carolina. As Lucas saw things, the state law banning construction on the coast amounted to an unlawful taking of his property. When a government formally seizes land through condemnation, a landowner is constitutionally entitled to receive just compensation. What Lucas claimed was that the state law, though not technically seizing his land, had the same economic effect because it deprived him of the right to use the land in the only way economically feasible.

Lucas's case was an example of an alleged regulatory taking—a land-use regulation that disrupts ownership rights so much that it is tantamount to physical confiscation and hence, like physical confiscation, triggers the government's obligation to pay. Takings claims such as these are worrisome to communities and rightfully so, given the underlying risk of a severe monetary judgment. So worrisome are they, in fact, that many communities are reluctant to impose new land-use rules. Unsure of where they stand legally and not wanting to undercut an institution as vital as private property ownership, communities stand idle as the land degrades further. Such impasses are unfortunate and dangerous, and they need to be circumvented if the work of promoting land health is to proceed. Voluntary measures are helpful and much needed, but it is unfair for those who act responsibly to be compelled to share a landscape with others who are dragging it down. In the end, communities simply must have the power to halt harmful activities and to protect the land's carrying capacity.

Communities concerned about the potential for takings claims can take several steps to minimize their occurrence. One such step is to avoid enacting laws that interfere with existing land-use activities, particularly laws that require owners to tear down existing buildings or that otherwise interfere with the use of existing structures. If land alteration is likely to damage the land's health, laws banning it need to be put in place before the alteration takes place. Another step to avoid takings problems is to ensure that new laws don't interfere with the rights of landowners to exclude unwanted people. A law that prevents landowners from ousting trespassers will almost always amount to a taking.

As communities protect natural areas, they'll be tempted to open up those areas to public recreational use, but that temptation should be resisted. Promotion of land health doesn't require the public to have access to private lands, and the less invasive new regulations are, the more likely landowners will be to accept them. Aside from these steps, local governments can reduce takings problems by working hard to ensure that landowners understand the reasons for new laws and have meaningful chances to participate in the law-making process.

Inevitably, though, no matter how gradual, sensitive, and inclusive they are in their reform of ownership rules, some landowners will complain of mistreatment. As discussed earlier, one of the more valid landowner complaints is likely to arise when a law distributes burdens among landowners in an unfair way, restricting what some can do while leaving others unaffected. A complaint such as this derives not from a regulation's lack of merit but from its unequal application.

Communities must strive to treat like landowners alike, allocating burdens as fairly as possible among owners of ecologically similar lands. If drainage practices need to change, for instance, or if wildlife habitat needs to be protected, the burdens of meeting these needs shouldn't rest on just a few. Complaints of unequal treatment, however, are meritorious only when the lands involved are ecologically similar. There's no unfairness, for instance, when plowing is curtailed on a hillside but not on nearby flat land. In many cases, claims of unfairness will in fact seek to compare ecologically dissimilar lands; such claims need to be discounted. As property laws are brought more in line with the land's natural features, the bundle of rights landowners possess will increasingly vary from tract to tract. But such differences in rights are defensible as long as the tracts of land are ecologically different in meaningful ways.

One often heard complaint is that land-use restrictions are unfair to landowners because it is the public that benefits from the restrictions, and therefore the public should pay the costs of implementation. Opponents of land-use restrictions use this argument regularly; it has become a staple, for instance, of the American Farm Bureau Federation, which seeks to protect farmers from all coercive environmental laws. An analogy is drawn between land-use restrictions and programs such as national defense, for which the public pays the costs. That analogy, though, overlooks a vital difference. Polluting is a harmful activity, and it's fair for a community to demand that a polluter halt that harm, even though the community as a whole will enjoy the benefit. Similarly, landowners who cause downstream flooding can be told to change their ways, without being paid by those whose land is flooded. And the public at large might well benefit when remaining wildlife habitat is spared from destruction, but the cause of the underlying problem has little directly to do with the public. The problem is caused by landowners, and it's reasonable to ask them to remedy it.

There are times, of course, when the public should pay for land-use limits. Generally speaking, though, this is the case only when a landowner is asked to go beyond the avoidance of harm to perform a service for the community that owners of similar land aren't asked to perform. For example, compensation may be appropriate when an open-space ordinance bans development on one parcel of land while allowing it on identical land nearby: If the development activity were truly harmful, the community would ban it in both places. On the other hand, when a land-use regulation covers all ecologically similar lands and reflects a clear decision that a particular activity is harmful, no compensation should be paid. A community need not pay when a newly enacted law protects *all* wetlands or requires *all* riparian landowners to protect stream banks. Even when laws are applied somewhat unevenly, however, no taking may have occurred, for communities deserve flexibility in deciding which lands are ecologically similar and in dealing with problems one step at a time.

The bottom line on takings claims, then, is this: Communities need to deal with such claims seriously, but in the end they need to act for the long-term common good, and that means insisting that landowners act responsibly and abide by evolving standards. If a community decides that a particular land use is harmful, it needs the courage to act on that judgment. And when the time comes to protect the land's carrying capacity, a community needs the strength to draw the line and stick to it. Developers and other landowners need to be told, plainly and firmly, that ecological harms are serious matters. They need to learn that as landowners, they'll be expected to help sustain ecosystem processes and native biodiversity. They need to understand, too, that permitted land-use options are increasingly coming to depend on the land itself and its peculiar ecological attributes. The old days of reshaping the land at will are nearing an end.

In time, as landowners realize how property laws are shifting, they can set their expectations accordingly. A developer who wants to engage in a particular land use will recognize that he or she needs to find land naturally suited for that particular endeavor. Eventually, as attitudes shift and the unknown becomes increasingly familiar, takings claims should become less common. Takings claims arise largely during times of transition, when property laws change and landowners are caught by surprise. As new laws settle in, problems should subside.

Ownership As Stewardship

When a community enacts a law telling a landowner to avoid harmful conduct, it isn't setting a lofty goal. Indeed, a no-harm rule is a rather low moral hurdle, one on which only the most insensitive landowners ought to stumble. Many landowners, fortunately, set higher goals, dedicating themselves to the promotion of a fertile, healthy land, the preservation of wildlife, and the nourishing of an aesthetically pleasing natural home. Many landowners do think about future generations and consider themselves not dominators of the land but stewards for owners yet to come. Aldo Leopold spoke to this subject and these people when he wrote about his land ethic. The question he posed wasn't about avoiding harm to his natural home; it was about pursuing excellence, about living as responsibly and ethically as possible. Communities as well as individuals can engage in discussions of excellent land use, asking the questions posed by Leopold and setting exacting standards for themselves.

Communities that embrace ambitious goals in their laws have various legal precedents they can turn to for support and inspiration. At law, owners of particular types of property have long been deemed to possess merely temporary use rights, with the property itself remaining a public asset. That idea dates back at least to ancient Roman law, which referred to such a right as a usufructory interest—a right to enjoy the fruits of an asset but not to damage or consume the asset itself. In American law, the idea remains alive and appears most prominently in the law of water. A person can own the right to use a body of water or to tap its flow but cannot own the flow itself. The water remains public property.

In the American West, where water is scarce and water law is more developed, the law insists that all water uses be beneficial to the public. Owners can tap water flows for a variety of purposes, including industrial and irrigation uses, but laws prohibit them from wasting water or using it in ways that produce no public benefit. In a few western states, notably California, the requirement of beneficial use is supplemented by a rule that all water uses must comport with evolving community standards of "reasonableness." Water users must pay attention to competing social needs and must even share the water when other important needs arise.

Beneficial use in water law isn't an isolated case in American jurisprudence; other legal precedents also exist that link private property ownership to the common good. One of the old adages of the common law is the Latin expression *Salus populi suprema lex esto*—"Let the welfare of the people be the supreme law," meaning the people as a collective whole, not the people as isolated individuals. The United States Supreme Court reflected this adage when it announced in a prominent nineteenth-century decision that "all property in this country is held under the implied obligation that the owner's use of it shall not be injurious to the community." Today, this public-spirited thinking is present in a body of law known as the public trust doctrine. That doctrine dates back to old Roman law, to Justinian's *Institutes*, which designated certain resources—"the air, running water, the sea and consequently the shores of the sea"—as things that were "common to humankind."

The public trust doctrine, long dormant, has gained new life over the past quarter century, particularly in cases involving land beneath navigable waterways and, in some states, beaches and tidal areas. Private parties may own and use these lands, but only in ways that don't unduly disrupt the various values that the trust promotes. Originally, those values centered on navigation, commerce, and fishing, but courts have updated the list to include recreational uses and a full range of ecological values. In California, the public trust doctrine also applies to private rights in water. In a prominent decision involving Mono Lake, the Supreme Court of California expanded the doctrine's application to include water flowing in nonnavigable streams. As a result of the decision, Los Angeles ultimately had to curtail its diversion of water from the tributaries feeding Mono Lake because of the grave ecological consequences the diversions were creating.

In the arid West, the doctrine of beneficial use is slowly being updated, as it should be, to put pressure on water uses that unduly harm the ecological integrity of waterways. When A. G. Chauncey & Co. began using the waters of Spring Creek in 1852, few settlers thought much about waterway health and few people saw harm in draining a river dry. People gained rights to use water in ways that benefited them economically but left waterways in sad shape. At the time, the uses seemed beneficial, and the community's definition of benefit was what counted.

Today, many current water uses no longer seem beneficial, particularly those that considerably distort water flows and degrade water quality. As a result, courts and agencies are being pressed to force changes in such practices. Many current water uses need to come to an end, particularly irrigation uses that generate little economic gain and cause grave harm to aquatic life and other stream values. The rate of change, however, has been slow, too slow for many observers, who have taken courts to task for standing by idly and failing to update ideas of beneficial-use more quickly.

Why the resistance to what seems like sensible reform? Many water users simply don't want to change their ways, any more than most polluters do, and although their voices alone might be overridden, they are strongly supported by libertarian, free-market advocates who dislike the idea of government telling people how to use what they own. Market mechanisms, they claim, are better able than government agencies and courts to bring about needed shifts in water-use patterns. Those who want a stream to support more ecologically sound uses, such as river rafting or trout fishing, the argument goes, ought to purchase the water they want from existing users. If the new water uses are so peculiarly public (e.g., supporting wildlife and reducing pollution) that no private group is likely to step forward and fund them, tax money should buy the needed water.

Opponents of this kind of free-market thinking have cast serious doubt on many of the assumptions that underlie this line of argument. There are, for instance, serious practical problems in moving water flows from place to place, and the whole idea of viewing water as merely a market commodity conveys harmful messages. The core issue, though, is one of moral legitimacy, a concern not only of water law but of property law as a whole. And the concern increases yearly as environmental degradation worsens and as property law, by permitting the damaging conduct, implicitly sanctions it. To understand this moral problem and grasp its significance, one needs to back up and recognize what private property ownership ultimately entails—what it means for a person to control a part of Earth when others challenge what he or she is doing.

As many people see it, private property ownership is fundamentally about the right to be left alone. But most property owners don't really want the community to leave them alone; they want the community to be on their side. When trespassers come, they want the community's police to come and protect them. When a dispute arises with a neighbor, they want the community's courts to defend their rights. And when a neighbor engages in a land use that interferes with their activities, they might even want the courts and police to halt what the neighbor is doing. An owner like this isn't asking to be left alone.

More aptly, private property ownership is understood as a form of community-sanctioned power, exercised against the rest of the world at a private owner's request. Given this reality, property law needs to be kept up to date so that it reflects contemporary ideas of what is fair and socially acceptable. It makes no sense, that is, for a community to offer aid to a landowner who wants to disturb the community's well-being. To remain legitimate over time, land-ownership norms need to bend and take on new shapes as communal values and circumstances evolve.

When property regimes become outdated, their legitimacy erodes and they become divisive forces within a community. Something is gravely wrong when the law vests private landowners with the power to impose harm without consequence or when it allows them to abuse and undermine things the community has come to treasure. The prospect of this happening becomes both more likely and more ominous when holders of private property rights are politically powerful enough to resist legal change.

An illustration of outdated property rules can be found in the harmful practices that gave rise to the civil rights legislation of the 1960s. In much of the United States, particularly in the South, owners of restaurants and motels engaged in overt racial discrimination. As property owners, they had the right to do so, and communities defended them with their police forces and courts. That discrimination, however, greatly harmed members of racial minority groups traveling around the country, and the national community reacted with moral outrage. Congress responded by passing civil rights laws that banned discrimination, thus bringing property laws more in line with public sentiment. Some property owners rebelled, claiming their property rights were being altered, and they were right. Before the new laws, landowners had the right to discriminate; after the laws, they did not. Their rights were indeed diminished, and precisely because the old laws had become outdated. Motel owners could have been paid to stop discriminating, and perhaps there was a time when payment appeared sensible. But by the 1960s, that solution was no longer just. It was recognized that racial discrimination was simply wrong and laws needed to change. To the community, it was no longer morally acceptable for state power to support racial discrimination.

A second example of outdated rules arose in eastern Kentucky, where badly polluted rivers and degraded communities bespeak the effects of strip mining. During the first half of the twentieth century, mining companies that held "broad form" coal leases were afforded the right to destroy the land in their race to strip-mine coal. Simply by owning the underlying coal, they were entitled to bulldoze private homes on the surface and even entire towns, with no concern for surrounding communities or residents downstream. By the 1960s, that form of private landownership appeared illegitimate to most Kentucky citizens, and many had become angry with government for bending to miners' wishes. Moral outrage increased, and property ownership laws finally changed. Today, mining companies are subject to greater regulation and must pay for the surface damage they cause.

As western water law continues to allow water uses that degrade rivers and threaten aquatic life, it inches closer to becoming like the racial discrimination and strip mining cases: Its legitimacy, morally and politically, gets weaker and weaker. Over the decades, water law has indeed changed as circumstances and cultural values have evolved. Still, more change is needed if the law is to avoid becoming a source of state-sanctioned ecological harm. In the case of damaging water uses, as with southern motels and Kentucky strip miners, the complaint is not about the distribution of property rights among people—a matter that markets might address. It's about the meaning of property ownership itself, about the power that private ownership entails.

Communities, in sum, have not only the power but also the duty to reshape landownership laws so that they reflect evolving community sentiment, banning destructive resource-use practices, whether to water, land, or other elements of nature's fabric. They need to set appropriate standards for landowner behavior and to take action when those standards aren't met. As land health becomes a more intentional goal, communities are likely to exercise new powers and draft new rules that are more attentive of the land, rules that imitate nature as the work of Wes Jackson does, rules that require owners to listen to the land and tailor their practices to sustain its long-term health.

Chapter 9

Promoting Land Health

FOR LANDSCAPES to become healthier, people need to alter their ways—their land-use practices, their consumption patterns, and their pollution-generating activities. Such changes don't come easily, a reality that few people know as well as Jim McMahon, a veteran promoter of land health. McMahon understands the kinds of shifts that are needed today, particularly in rural communities like his own. And he can describe the hard work that first needs to occur: the research, education, discussion, and planning. Most of all, though, he can talk about the patience that needs to be stockpiled, drawn on, and periodically replenished if a community-based conservation effort is to have hope of success.

McMahon has gained his most recent experience in the watershed of the Mackinaw River, a tributary of the Illinois River that ends south of Peoria. The Mackinaw winds for 130 miles through the Illinois countryside, draining an area of 744,000 acres. Nearly

all the land is owned by farmers, and an astonishing 87 percent of
it is tilled. In 1993, The Nature Conservancy of Illinois selected
the Mackinaw as a trial site for citizen-run conservation work. The
following year, McMahon was brought in to run the project,
funded with money from the state's environmental protection
agency and aided by scientists from its natural history and water
surveys. McMahon had hardly arrived when he realized how daunting the challenges were. Few people welcomed him; few could
even grasp what he had in mind. As he looks back today, he is surprised he had the perseverance to continue.

LISTENING AND TALKING

The Nature Conservancy came to the Mackinaw because the river
suffered from problems common to most Illinois waterways.
Sediment loads in the river were high, causing mussels and fish to
die. Some of the river's sediment came from unprotected farm
fields and reflected losses of valuable topsoil. Other sediment came
from stream-bank erosion, which was exacerbated by regional
drainage practices. As rainwater hit farm fields, it moved quickly
through subsurface drainage tiles, creating a powerful flow that
cut into the river's banks. The resulting high water levels created
downstream flooding and put many farm fields underwater. Flooding was worsened by loss of wetlands, removal of floodplain vegetation, and replacement of pastures and hayfields with even more
tilled fields for corn and soybeans. Chemical contaminants were
less of a problem than in most Illinois rivers, and the state considered the water quality of the Mackinaw high. Still, pollution was
sufficiently bad that the river had lost one-fourth of its fish and
mussel species since the 1950s. Monitoring of the river's water
quality was infrequent and was rarely done at peak flow times, when
spring rains carried pesticides and fertilizers off newly sprayed
farm fields.

    These problems all made the Mackinaw a typical regional waterway and hence a good site for conservation work. Less typical but also appealing was the river's unusual geological history and physical structure. The Mackinaw's watershed had been formed by withdrawing Ice Age glaciers, which left behind an extended moraine of boulders. Today, the river flows along the boulders and is more stable because of them. With these geologic features, the river possesses a strong aesthetic appeal, and its gravel-bottomed sections support fishes not found in typical dirt-lined waterways. Local residents enjoy the river and feel attached to it. It is a part of their home and a part of who they are.

Even so, when The Nature Conservancy first arrived, local people had little regard for the river's aquatic diversity and seemed unconcerned about its imperiled species, particularly its endangered mussels. Nature Conservancy personnel and McMahon soon realized that biological preservation didn't mean nearly as much to local farmers as did the flooding problem. Sensitive to the farmers' perspectives, McMahon spent his first six months on the job simply listening. Back and forth he traveled across the watershed, talking to landowners and hearing how they perceived the river. He offered information about problems and probable causes, but only to those who wanted it. He quickly learned that nothing would happen until local people became less distrustful of him and the Conservancy. Most people assumed that The Nature Conservancy had come to their area to criticize them and tell them what to do, trampling on private property rights in the process.

Given these fears, McMahon proceeded as patiently and humbly as he could. He made sure he had good science to draw on, knowing that if he did not, his best efforts would soon unravel. He and his family moved to the watershed so he could relate to people as one of their neighbors. As he traveled, McMahon encouraged people to look closely at the river. He took them to spots where they could learn for themselves about altered water flows and unprotected floodplains. He organized tours so that upstream landowners could see how farmland downstream was impaired by poor water management, land owned by farmers just like themselves. Many upstream owners, he found out, had never really been downstream. They didn't know what was happening there, just as downstream owners didn't realize how their problems were linked to those of farmers upstream, sometimes their friends and relatives.

McMahon initially interacted with a group of fifteen landowners who had responded to The Nature Conservancy's call for local volunteers to work on the river. The fifteen who signed on, all farmers living near the river, formed a committee and began to learn about the river. With McMahon serving as its sixteenth member, the group designed a process for preparing a watershed plan and soon hired a facilitator, Larry Huggins, with The Nature Conservancy footing the bill. At Huggins's suggestion, the group doubled its size and became more diverse by including sportsmen, local government officials, and drainage district commissioners, though farmers remained in the majority. The enlarged group became known as the Planning Team, with the original sixteen serving as the Executive Committee.

It wasn't long before McMahon could feel changes in the air. The problems, to be sure, all remained. No land uses had changed; no plans had been drawn up. But people were treating him differently and saying surprising things. Some talked about the benefits that could come from restoring wetlands. Others spoke knowingly of the river's hydrology and the ill effects associated with farm drainage. People were noticing floodplains that weren't protected by vegetation and farm fields that were plowed right to ditch's edge. And they were expressing frustration with arbitrary political boundaries. People were also commenting on McMahon himself. He wasn't telling them what to do, they noted with surprise; he was a reasonable guy, open-minded and anxious to learn along with them.

At the same time, Diane Rudin of The Nature Conservancy worked with the larger watershed community. Her specialty was community education, and she, too, crossed the watershed again and again, meeting with groups in schools, meeting halls, and churches, talking about the watershed and telling them about the Planning Team's efforts. She also supplied information to the news media, and interest there became intense. Before long, articles were appearing in local newspapers at the rate of two per week. Word of the project was getting out.

Aided by Huggins, the Planning Team identified its land-use goals and began incorporating them into a watershed plan. The harder the team members worked, the more inclined they became toward change. Slowest to come around were the two drainage district commissioners on the team, to no one's surprise. Poorly drained land, they had always thought, was an affront to any good farmer. Rainwater was managed by moving it downstream as rapidly as possible; flooding was handled by building levees higher and higher. Yet gradually even the commissioners began to revise their thinking.

As the work of the Planning Team progressed, its goals became increasingly ambitious. By 1997, four years into the project, vague ideas had become precise numbers, and a draft plan had taken shape. To improve water quality and reduce flooding, 7,500 acres of upland wetlands would need restoration. To trap sediment and retain water, 15,000 acres of floodplain were proposed for revegetation. An additional 15,000 acres of land were needed in prairie or forest. Most ambitiously, restoration and stream-bank protection were needed along a full 700 miles of the Mackinaw River's main corridor and its many small tributaries. In addition, individual farmers would be asked to embrace various low-impact practices such as no-till cultivation and to build structures such as terraces and detention basins.

As the Planning Team worked, it inevitably interacted closely with the U.S. Department of Agriculture. The USDA was a powerful force on the landscape, having encouraged most of the landscape changes over the previous half century. With the support of Congress, the agency had not only advocated extensive drainage

but also provided money to make it possible. It had pushed farmers
to simplify their crops, employ the latest chemicals, and plow the
last bits of tillable wildlife habitat. The agency had long worried
about soil erosion, yet even in the 1990s it was reluctant to accept
responsibility for impaired water quality and declining biodiversity. Even so, McMahon was anxious to reach out to the USDA
and gain its cooperation. Without its support, he knew, the project
would very likely stall.

Also important on the local scene was the American Farm
Bureau Federation, the chief organization representing farm interests. The Farm Bureau had become more focused and strident
late in the century, and it resisted claims that high-tech farming
created serious environmental problems. On water issues, it endorsed the drainage district mentality, and to ward off environmental regulation it waved high the property rights flag. It even
rented billboard space to discredit the aims and dedication of environmental groups. Still, the Farm Bureau stood solidly in favor of
volunteer programs to address environmental issues. Since Mc-
Mahon had no thought of coercive measures and was himself respectful of property rights, he approached the Farm Bureau as a
potential ally.

By April 1997, the draft plan was complete though it remained
vague as to where changes would occur, who would pay for them,
and how they would be initiated. At that point, the Planning Team
ceased its work, leaving the Executive Committee to publicize the
plan, oversee demonstration projects, and solicit support. As implementation began, however, the plan quickly met with resistance
stemming from ingrained attitudes and values. Planning Team
members had learned and embraced new ideas, but community
members who were outside the process remained unenlightened.
Drainage district commissioners returned to their constituents
flush with new ideas only to find that prevailing ideas and values
were as entrenched as ever. The virtues of ideas that made sense to
Planning Team members were not at all apparent to landowners
who hadn't done the studying and thinking.

To get matters moving, the Executive Committee initiated fifteen demonstration projects dispersed around the watershed. Five wetlands were constructed or restored, and three detention ponds were constructed. Stream-bank reaches were protected and forest restoration projects begun. These projects would help get the message out, both about the project and about how land uses and drainage practices were related to water quality and flooding problems. Yet real progress would depend on more fundamental shifts in the ways people experienced the land. People needed to see the many ill effects of overengineering; they needed to feel how unnatural and unhealthy the waterway had become, in large part due to changes in agricultural practices. So simplified had modern farm practices become that woodlots and wetlands no longer had an economic function on the family farm, and the land's health suffered because of it. Too many farmers had lost touch with the pleasures of a diverse, healthy land. Somehow they needed to recover their childhood memories of trapping muskrats in the nearby wetland, searching the woods for mushrooms, sailing boats on the farm pond, or watching meadowlarks and bobolinks in the pasture. Memories of a different, richer landscape were out there, if only they could be tapped.

Promoting Local Work

The work Jim McMahon and his colleagues are doing along the Mackinaw River is as vital and promising as any conservation work now going on. Although it is only beginning, their work has progressed and already has a solid foundation. Still, as McMahon puts it, this is work for the long-winded, for people who can toil year after year, unsure of the path yet trusting that a healthier land lies ahead. One day, he hopes, the river's flow will moderate to more natural levels, water quality will improve, soil will stay in place, and environmentally sensitive aquatic species will thrive. People living in the watershed will be aware of their links to the river and will think of their watershed in holistic terms. Landowners will confine themselves to land uses that are appropriate in nature's terms and will shoulder their fair share of landscape-scale duties, such as providing room for wildlife and sustaining ecological processes.

But landscapes can regain their health only if the will exists locally. As the Mackinaw River experience shows, local people must be active participants in the process of change. Not everyone needs to participate, of course, but enough people and enough different kinds of people need to for the effort to become a community-wide undertaking. Good science must be part of that work, and local people can usefully participate in the data collection. With minimal training and supervision ordinary citizens can spot instances of soil erosion and gather data on water quality and wildlife populations. People who see their land from this more analytical perspective tend to be more protective of it. In some instances, local people possess specialized knowledge about the land. Researchers who began studying wolves, for instance, found that local trappers knew more than anyone about wolf behavior.

Promotion of land health will also require local citizens to consider the ethical aspects of their life on the land, recognizing the limits of science and human knowledge and acting cautiously in the face of that ignorance. With this recognition will come a number of more broad-ranging questions: How much respect do other species deserve, and how far should humans bend to accommodate them? If we are stewards of the land for people yet to come, what claims do later generations have, and how should those now living respect those claims? Aesthetic questions might also arise: How can the beauty of nature be brought into people's lives, and what kinds of landscapes do people want to inhabit?

Plainly, the achievement of land health is not a onetime task but an ongoing process requiring a great deal of work. In particular communities, work to promote land health will take many forms and proceed along varied lines, resisting efforts to turn it into a predictable process with established routines. It will be messier than that, and yet it will be more flexible and vibrant because of its messiness. All the work needs to fit together into a community-based regimen or practice, tailored to each particular landscape and to the specific needs and circumstances of local people.

The achievement of land health will require input from research centers, input that can be modified according to a community's needs. The Land Institute's work offers a leading example here, as do the research of the Rocky Mountain Institute on solar energy and energy conservation and the work of Appalachia Science in the Public Interest on new forestry methods and ecologically sound forest economies. If modern agricultural methods, for instance, are as wrongheaded as Wes Jackson and others think, the entire enterprise must be revisited, a process local people simply can't undertake alone. People along the Mackinaw River can treat the most obvious symptoms of poor land health by plugging drainage lines and constructing wetlands. But to go further, to fundamentally reconsider farming as it's now practiced, will require different skills and greater sophistication.

One of the sad realities faced by those working toward a new land ethic is the lack of support from institutions, including those that ought to be in the forefront of change. Although state environmental protection agencies endorse the idea of bottom-up, community-based conservation, they tend to operate on too large a scale, focusing their efforts on rivers that are too large for citizens to feel both protective of and sufficiently empowered to save. State agency officials also resist giving up control and tend not to understand how vital it is for citizens to get involved. When Jim McMahon talked to people along the Mackinaw, he sought their views as community members and landowners, not because they headed stakeholder organizations. Drainage district commissioners were brought in because they wielded power, but they, too, were expected to participate as citizens and to rethink their assumptions and positions.

Overall, people are suspicious of government, particularly above the local level, and greet with skepticism any claim that the government might want to empower rather than control them. They become passive or resistant when government agencies assert themselves, reacting enthusiastically only when money can be gained for pet local projects. Is it therefore surprising that most government-run projects are viewed more as pork-barrel politics than as meritorious endeavors?

Practical support for community-based conservation also remains weak among universities, which typically embrace global thinking and severely discount local community life. Because universities are presumed to serve students best by preparing them for urban life in a faraway place, most students depart with specialized skills that have little bearing on local lands and local communities. Even at state universities, students may learn nothing about the soils, waters, ecosystems, and biological heritage of their state. When universities do teach conservation, it is treated as a specialty, in no way central to a general education. Even more alien to educators is the proposal of Wes Jackson that universities offer majors in homecoming, helping students learn skills to take back home, whether to small towns or inner-city neighborhoods.

CIVIC ENGAGEMENT

Along with good science, the birth of a new land ethic depends on good processes for getting people together and encouraging deliberation. People need to participate as well-rounded citizens, committed to the long-term common good. This kind of civic engagement has a long and honorable tradition in the United States. Thomas Jefferson had it in mind when he talked about the independent virtuous citizen. Landownership, Jefferson believed, encouraged public virtue. Landowners, he thought, would be secure enough economically and respected enough socially to rise above self-interest and address matters of common concern.

Getting people to deliberate collectively, however, represents a major challenge. Most group discussions focus on short-term strategies—on specific policies to pursue, such as building a dam or enacting a zoning ordinance—with no real consideration of desired long-term aims such as leaving a landscape ecologically sound for future generations. Rarely are the bigger issues even mentioned. Moreover, many times the only public venues for discussion are government hearings, which are poorly designed for civic engagement. People who attend such gatherings don't talk with and listen to one another; they talk to government officials or hearing officers at the front of the room. Views are formed in advance, and no time is set aside for reflection and response. Inevitably, citizens develop the sense that they stand opposed to government and in competition with neighbors rather than allied with others seeking a common good.

Government boundaries pose another problem for promoters of land health. Jim McMahon encountered this obstacle as soon as he began work on the Mackinaw. As is the case in other regions of the former Northwest Territory, the Mackinaw's watershed is divided into square sections and townships. People think of themselves as residents of counties and townships, not as occupants of drainage basins or other natural features. McMahon had to get people to think in different terms, to realign their loyalties a bit and pay attention to natural rather than artificial boundaries. Paradoxically, though, McMahon might have had even more trouble if a watershed-based government had already been in existence when he arrived. He might have been dismissed as just another government critic and castigated for interfering. But McMahon was not hamstrung in this way. In fact, by focusing on the entire watershed, McMahon was cutting against existing ways of doing business, and his work was more novel and visible because of it.

Still, McMahon found that most people he encountered readily embraced government-drawn boundaries. Before residents could think constructively about the Mackinaw, they had to overcome their ingrained individualism and think in more communitarian terms. A community spirit did exist, yet it rested on ideas of voluntarism and tolerance. Missing was a sense of common unity that gave rise to community-wide decision making. Mackinaw residents had no tradition of joint citizen action comparable to the traditions in Europe that centered on management of the village commons. They weren't accustomed to making joint decisions that imposed obligations on themselves as community members.

To the people along the Mackinaw, the term *community* carried various meanings. Often the term did refer to relationships based on place, but the places typically were towns and other political units rather than natural features. Still, McMahon sensed that he had something to work with. A strong sense of community was essential, he knew, for without it landowners simply wouldn't take seriously any conception of a common good. They might halt any visible harmful practices, but without a holistic perspective, they would be unlikely to grapple with deeper ethical challenges.

McMahon had no illusion that community building would be easy, particularly among people so influenced by the competitive market spirit. He knew, too, that the concept of community had become so vague and flexible that many people wondered what the term meant and whether community even existed in a meaningful way. But McMahon had one powerful tool on his side, something he could point to as a tangible reality, linking people together: the Mackinaw River itself. Maps showed the river's watershed, and people could see clearly how nature tied them together. The encompassing nature of watersheds, in fact, had a lot to do with The Nature Conservancy's decision to employ a waterway focus for its community-based work. Another factor was that people tend to care about rivers. River conservation has an emotional and aesthetic appeal that activities such as soil conservation have never engendered. Older people in particular often have fond memories associated with rivers and aquatic life, memories from days when the river was healthier and more beautiful. Along the Mackinaw, nearly all environmental problems other than air pollution and atmospheric contamination show up in the river, directly or indirectly. Conversely, as the river heals, the entire land community improves.

Had McMahon's work taken him to another part of the country, his community-based conservation effort might have focused instead on protecting other parts of nature—an ecological community like the Everglades, for example, or a large animal like the grizzly bear or condor. Illinois's landscape, however, has been altered so drastically that imperiled ecosystems exist only as small fragments. Large native animals that were disturbed by human activities are all long gone, and the state's remaining endangered species aren't the kind to serve as community-organizing devices. Another focus was needed, and rivers offered the obvious choice.

Watershed maps in hand, Jim McMahon was able to talk to people about the river community. With the river, he had a place to begin. People along the Mackinaw, he knew, believed that land-use issues were best addressed at the local level. What they lacked most were reasons to get together and talk. Without an awareness of local problems, they weren't likely to see a need for change; without opportunities to talk and exchange ideas and hopes, they weren't likely to take a longer perspective and elevate their ethical goals. By inclination as well as necessity, McMahon had faith in the local people. As he came to phrase his guiding wisdom, "If you give good people good information, they will make great decisions."

BEYOND THE MACKINAW

In its limited abilities to deal with problems, the Mackinaw River's human community differs little from communities everywhere. The river makes the watershed a distinct community, but just as the river is fed by tributaries and flows into larger waterways, the watershed is joined by surrounding communities and helps compose much larger ones, including the national and global commu-

nities. Thus, the Mackinaw cannot be viewed in isolation but must
be assessed as a component of larger ecosystems. What happens to
the Mackinaw spills over into the Illinois River, which in turn dis-
charges into the Mississippi River, which in turn empties into the
Gulf of Mexico, and so on, according to the rules of the planet's
water cycle. Thinking in terms of downstream consequences
pushes communities to ask a number of hard questions. What happens when a river empties into another? Is the water free of
human-caused contaminants? Is its flow roughly comparable to a
natural flow, and if not, might floods and droughts ensue? Similar
questions can be asked about a watershed's wildlife and even its
vegetative communities. Wandering animals don't respect watershed boundaries, nor do ecological disturbances such as fires,
storms, and pest invasions. Land-use patterns in one watershed
can affect plant and animal life in adjacent areas.

In the presence of such connections, standards need to be set so
that no one community can act in ways that degrade surrounding
communities. Standards should also be set that take future generations into account, focusing on such matters as soil conservation
and biodiversity protection. Higher levels of government play a legitimate and often indispensable role in setting these standards,
for it is too easy for small communities to limit themselves to an
inward focus, ignoring their links to surrounding lands. Higher
levels of government may also be needed to help local people get
started with conservation work when groups such as The Nature
Conservancy aren't around and to intervene if their work doesn't
succeed.

Inevitably, the promotion of a healthy land will involve all levels
of government. Industrial pollution, for example, requires federal-
level action, even in states with aggressive environmental protection agencies. When it comes to global climate change, ozone
depletion, and control of biological pests, multinational action is
required. Generally speaking, environmental problems should be
addressed at the lowest level of government that is willing and

competent to deal with a problem, with citizens involved when-ever possible. This general principle, though, merely provides a starting point for what needs to be a pragmatic inquiry into the best way to divide responsibilities and power among different lev-els of government.

As the Mackinaw River project demonstrates, getting started at the local level isn't always easy. Local people don't always know how resources ought to be used, nor are they always aware of sub-tle but insidious problems. In addition, local processes are too eas-ily dominated by particular interests bent on resource exploitation, such as timber cutters, miners, or grazers. Communities domi-nated by timber clear-cutters are transient and profit oriented by their very nature, with leaders who move on when the exploitation is complete. Moreover, local government bodies can have a pre-determined agenda when they're created for a single purpose. A drainage district created to get water downstream as rapidly as possible is inclined to act irresponsibly, especially when it's domi-nated by landowners with land to drain. Because government agen-cies such as this don't accurately reflect overall community inter-ests and values and rarely deliberate on the common good, they need to take orders from government agencies that do.

At the state and federal levels, irresponsibility is bred by bu-reaucratization, with environmental problems sent to one agency while other agencies charge ahead. Departments of agriculture typically promote large-scale farming, with little concern for its adverse effects. Transportation agencies are as bad or worse. At the federal level, the U.S. Department of Interior's Bureau of Land Management is so dominated by grazing and mining interests that it gives the entire idea of public land management a bad name. Like the BLM, most federal agencies show, at best, sporadic inter-est in respecting the spirit of environmental laws. Environmental impact statements often are prepared only when they're required by law, not because agencies find them useful. Clear-cutting in the national forests occurs in stark disregard of congressional instructions to clear-cut only when environmental effects are benign and when clear-cutting is otherwise "optimal."

Ultimately, determining the appropriate level of environmental decision making eludes an easy answer. All other things being equal, local people should be empowered to handle problems that are within their capabilities. Beyond that, government agencies with broad goals and widespread representation should get the nod over those with a narrow focus and obvious ties to special-interest groups. And agencies with deliberative processes or processes that entail meaningful public participation should be favored over those that employ streamlined, hierarchical modes of making decisions.

Despite those who might wish otherwise, high levels of government have vital work to perform. No small community can take on a multinational corporation, any more than it can clean up a major river. And businesses sometimes play one community against another, dangling jobs in front of desiring eyes on the condition that they receive free rein to degrade local lands. Moreover, local communities can't realistically interfere with interstate commerce by banning products with excessive packaging or setting standards for vehicle emissions. Nor, realistically, can they subject local businesses to standards of performance so costly that they can't reasonably compete with businesses elsewhere. Recognizing this reality, Congress in the early 1970s insisted on nationwide pollution-control standards on the assumption that if states and local communities had the power to weaken standards, they'd be hard-pressed to do so, even against their will.

Although some complain that state and federal mandates interfere with local autonomy, the reality is that higher levels of government are needed to protect local efforts from outside forces. Without help from above, community-based efforts would face an impossible battle. Community members shouldn't have to worry that local businesses will flee to places where land health isn't taken seriously. Nor should they have to worry that local farmers or consumers will import chemicals that endanger the community's health. To remove environmental laws put in place by higher governments is often to weaken local power, not strengthen it.

CONNECTING THE PIECES

When communities and governments work together to promote land health, the effect is not to erase boundaries as much as to connect the pieces, the townships and counties, the private parcels and separate watersheds. The boundaries remain in place, focusing efforts and marking the limits of particularized care, but people see through and beyond them. It is not the land that is bounded but the people living and working on the land.

Community efforts to promote land health add a logical next step to the visions of good stewardship offered by Aldo Leopold and Wendell Berry. Leopold spoke of the responsible individual whose use of the land was guided by an organic vision, one that blends ecology, ethics, and aesthetics. Wendell Berry built on that base in his portrayal of Mat Feltner, a man so connected to his community and to past and future generations that his personal goals fit snugly with the common good. Mat was a solid community member, attached to his bounded farm but connected firmly with everything around him.

What Mat and his neighborhood lacked were powerful and orderly ways of organizing their efforts as a community to promote the health of their chosen natural home. They needed better tools to curtail destructive activities of local residents who simply weren't as responsible as Mat, and they needed assistance with matters that were scientifically complex. Most of all, though, they needed help in defending themselves against the allure, the ill effects, and the sheer power of the commodity-focused market.

In 1852 and 1853, A. G. Chauncey & Co. and Spring Creek Water and Mining Co. had no trouble talking about business. Negotiating as profit-oriented enterprises, they made deals that benefited them both. But when the river's water ran short, they went head to head as competitors, each hoping to win. No sense of common interest encouraged them to act in concert. So far as the record reflects, they never talked about their shared home, the community of the Spring Creek watershed. Perhaps neither side even thought of it. And if they talked about the long term or about the health of the watershed, that, too, escaped the court's report.

Had the businesses expanded their discussions, they might have taken up issues such as these. But they considered themselves competitors, not cooperators, and when the court handed down its ruling, one side won and the other side lost. While they fought, the river itself suffered.

There is a sadness, a wistful air, about Frost's "Mending Wall" that is hard to identify at first. Welling up within the narrator is a longing that is never fulfilled. Nature doesn't need this stone wall, the narrator has figured out. Boundaries are human creations, reflecting human needs. But what are those needs, he implicitly asks, and how important are they? Why is it that people build fences, whether of stone or of the imagination? The narrator wants the fence to come down, yet his goal remains elusive. He fears even to speak of it.

The stone wall exists, we know, not really to bound the land but to mark the boundaries the farmers have imposed on themselves and their imaginations. Like all people, these farmers have their limits. They can know and love only a human-sized piece of land. Their longing for territory is ingrained, and so is their attachment to private property. They are prepared to share work and to cooperate, but the cooperation needs to occur in dignifying ways. Perhaps the farmers are flawed souls—fallen and overly proud ones, the religious tradition might say—particularly the stubborn neighbor who can speak only of good fences. Yet they are identifiably human all the same. The nature within them is human nature, the stuff of real communities.

By poem's end, the sadness remains, not because the wall remains and the mending work continues but because the narrator never had the courage to speak up. Had his subject been trivial, the poem's sadness might easily be dismissed. But the narrator's unspoken point was an important one: Nature is an unbounded whole, he wanted to say; it doesn't come in human-sized pieces. Boundaries are unnatural, however useful they are for people. The land is not just a place for humans to carve up and inhabit. It is more than that and other than that.

As readers, we can only speculate what might have happened had the narrator spoken up, just as we're left to wonder what might have ensued had A. G. Chauncey and Spring Creek Co. recognized their shared interests. The stone wall probably wouldn't have come down, but the narrator's comment might have led to something else, to a recognition of other ways in which the neighbors were linked and to further means of cooperation. And so the sadness of the poem is not just about unspoken hopes. It is about cooperation that might have happened and did not.

ONE OF THE towns in the Mackinaw River's watershed is tiny Sibley, home to just a few hundred people. As Jim McMahon and the Executive Committee began identifying possible pilot projects, they talked with Sibley leaders about constructing a 3,000-acre wetland complex outside town. Aside from its ecological benefits, a wetland offered prospects for nature tourism by birders and hunters who would be attracted to the waterfowl. As the discussions continued, committee members learned of a problem Sibley had long had with its modest 15-acre pond, formed thousands of years ago by the last retreating glacier. The water body, which ap-

170 *Boundless People, Boundless Lands*

peared on few maps and whose existence was known only to a few locals, was filling with silt from surrounding farm fields. The solution, town officials said, was to dredge the pond. But dredging costs money. Applications were filled out and government grants sought, but money simply wasn't available for dredging. Each year, the situation worsened.

When Nature Conservancy staff members studied the matter, they found that the pond's watershed was only 80 acres in size. And aside from the pond itself, a large portion of the watershed was owned by a single farmer, who tilled his land annually as did most Illinois farmers. Knowing what they did, Conservancy staff members asked the question that to them seemed obvious: What had the farmer said when told about the problem? How had he responded when asked to change his tillage practices?

The answer that came back would have surprised neither Robert Frost nor the California judiciary of the gold-rush era. Town representatives, it turned out, had never talked to the farmer. They had never confronted him with the problem or raised the possibility of change.

Conservancy staff members quickly approached the farmer and asked him about enrolling the 80 acres in the federal conservation reserve program as a means of halting erosion.

Sounded like a good idea, the farmer said.

Coda

Toward a Shared
Land Ethic

*It is a fact, patent both to my dog and myself, that at daybreak I am the
sole owner of all the acres I can walk over. It is not only boundaries that
disappear, but also the thought of being bounded.*   ALDO LEOPOLD

THINK IT A prime mark of a real gift," Justice Oliver Wendell
Holmes wrote, "to realize that any piece of the universe may be
made poetical if seen by a poet." Holmes presumably was speaking not of writing that depicts land merely in picturesque, landscape terms, but of writing that captures the inherent essence of a
place, writing that uncovers the sense of life within the land, that
portrays its hidden energy and its alluring mystique.

Holmes offered this comment after reading Willa Cather's *My
Ántonia*, a novel set in south-central Nebraska and based on the ex-

periences of Cather and her family. At the time of the story, the
early 1880s, the pioneering period was coming to an end, yet living
conditions remained primitive and the land was little developed.
Sod huts still dotted the plains, and farmers lived in isolation, sur-
rounded by a countryside that to many of them appeared empty,
desolate, and dreary. Like the Cather family, many Nebraska settlers had come from hilly, wooded lands back east, and the sharp
winds, prairie fires, and insect invasions made them think fondly of
their old homes. Driven to make a living, families rushed to claim
a well-marked quarter section of land and intently took to the task
of making the land produce.

As a young girl, though, and later as a writer, Cather wasn't pre-
occupied with such pragmatic needs. Where others saw worthless
prairie plants, she saw beauty. While others respected boundaries
and sought out unclaimed tracts, she soaked up the land as a whole.
Although the land had largely shifted to private ownership, much
of it was still untouched by the plow. The rolling alluvial plain
around the Cather homestead remained clothed in prairie grasses
and abounded in quail and prairie chickens.

It's hard to know what the nine-year-old Willa Cather thought
of the Nebraska plains when she first arrived, but a quarter century
later, in the opening pages of *My Ántonia*, she presents that land as
seen by her young fictional counterpart, Jim Borden. The heat of
summer has given way to the crispness of early fall. The prairie
plants are in seed, and many have turned from green to autumn
browns, deep blues, and rusts. "Everywhere, as far as the eye could
reach," Jim relates as he gazes toward the horizon, "there was
nothing but rough, shaggy red grass." "As I looked about me," he
recounts,

> *I felt that the grass was the country, as the water is the sea. The red
> of the grass made all the great prairie the color of wine-stains, or of
> certain seaweeds when they are first washed up. And there was so
> much motion in it; the whole country seemed, somehow, to be run-
> ning.*

To Jim, the land is alive with subtle energies, and he is moved by it and with it. "More than anything else," he relates, "I felt motion in the landscape; in the fresh, easy-blowing morning wind, and in the earth itself, as if the shaggy grass were a sort of loose hide, and underneath it herds of wild buffalo were galloping, galloping." Jim yearns to join himself with this shifting land, to have it envelop and consume him; he yearns, as he puts it, "to become a part of something entire, whether it is sun and air, or goodness and knowledge." "At any rate," he proposes, "that is happiness; to be dissolved into something complete and great."

American and other Western cultures have been overly inclined to divide the natural world into pieces and to see the land community not as a blurred mosaic of ecosystems but as a collection of homesteads, water flows, and natural resources. The same tendency toward division and separation shows up in the social realm, where human society is understood as a collection of individuals. But the more a society emphasizes boundaries—the more weight it gives to property lines and individual autonomy—the more it denigrates the natural and social fabrics. Boundaries have their uses, but once they are constructed and respected, they take on lives of their own, constricting the vision, understanding, and behavior of the people who've erected them. In all likelihood, the neighbor in Robert Frost's "Mending Wall" understood the land and his place on it far differently because of the stone wall and what the wall meant to him and his home culture.

On the eve of the new century, Americans are much in need of a more poetic sense of the land, a sense of its organic wholeness and beauty; its inner motion and energy, its subtle music and spirituality. To tend the land wisely is not just to use it efficiently; it is to recognize the land's sacredness and show it due respect.

When the land is rigidly divided, physically and in the minds and hearts of people, it becomes harder for people to experience the sense of boundlessness Aldo Leopold felt as he roamed the land with his dog at dawn, before the business day began and before human-created boundaries reasserted their potent influence.

It becomes harder, too, to sense the land as Willa Cather did, as a "loose hide," reverberating still from the galloping herds of buffalo that graced the land before hunters and fences put an end to their freedom, severing yet another of nature's links. Divided into pieces, the land no longer surrounds a person as an organic unity, a welcoming whole that invites a person to blend with it and contendedly become part of its cycles and mysteries.

A sense of boundlessness needs to undergird a new land ethic, an ethic not just for individuals but for gathered communities. The time must come when landowners concern themselves not just with a single parcel of land but with the landscape that includes it. For such an ethic to arise, communal reflection and discussion need to take place, as well as individual growth.

Several steps need to be taken if conservation and a new land ethic are to gain ground in the new century:

- Environmental policy needs to focus primarily on the land and other renewable natural resources. Pollution and toxic waste issues will remain important, and atmospheric problems will demand heightened attention. Yet across the country, land-use issues cry out for redress, issues relating to what Leopold deemed the fundamentals: the soil, water flows, biological diversity, and the integrity of ecological systems and processes. Drainage, erosion, soil degradation, runoff pollution, and similar specific issues need work. Most of all, though, landscape-level planning needs to begin, aimed at respecting the land's carrying capacity, preserving its beauty, and guaranteeing its health in perpetuity.

- Community-based conservation needs to assume center stage, along with other processes that get people involved as citizens. Work of this type will not be easy; indeed, it will be maddeningly slow and frustrating. But there is simply no alternative, not in a democratic culture so committed to liberty. What Jim McMahon and The Nature Conservancy are doing on the Mackinaw River needs to occur in every watershed and ecolog-

ical community across the land, along with higher-level work
focused on larger scales.

- A clear and specific goal is needed to guide and explain the conservation agenda, a holistic goal focused on community well-
being. Far better than sustainable development or sustainability
is the goal of land health, with *land* understood as the entire
land community and *health* understood in a way that mixes both
science and ethics. In pursuit of that goal, Wes Jackson's work
stands as a useful model—work that uses nature as the measure
and draws on its built-in wisdom.

- Boundaries on the land and in the human mind need to be re-
thought. In some cases, existing boundaries will need to be
erased and new ones, more imitative of nature, installed in their
place. More often, existing boundaries merely need to become
more permeable, like Mat Feltner's fence, so that life and responsibilities can flow through them. The chief challenge,
though, will be dealing with the cultural boundaries within people, getting people to see and then to cherish life's many interconnections. As the writer of Ecclesiastes put it, for a healthy
future, we must become "joined with all the living."

- The bundle of rights landowners possess needs reshaping so that
owners are required to use private property in ways consistent
with the land's health. Along with changes in laws, changes are
needed in the ways private property fits into the story of America as a land of opportunity and freedom. As a culture, America
needs to move beyond the myth of conquest and domination to
see private ownership as a matter of respecting the land and
using it in responsible ways. Only in this way will environmental laws appear consistent with core American values.

- In the messages it conveys and the arguments it presents, the
environmental movement needs to challenge the dominance of
individualism in modern culture—the dominance, that is, of
liberal autonomy and free-market ways of viewing the world as
a collection of pieces. As in the case of private property owner-

ship, the need is not to destroy the old—not to get rid of private property rights or to destroy individual liberty. The need is to shift back toward the middle, to a place where the community also counts.

- Finally, there is an indispensable need for good stories, stories about how people and land come together, about present generations joining hands with past and future ones, about people regaining intimacy and friendship with other species, about nature's inherent mystique and the limits of human knowledge, about the joys of communal life, and about the resettlement of the American land. New writers and storytellers need to join the tradition of Willa Cather, Wallace Stegner, Wendell Berry, and so many others. More stories must arise so that every pocket and corner of the country, as Holmes put it, "may be made poetical."

Envisioning a new land ethic is a matter of imagination and yearning far more than of science, economics, and law. Enough science is already available to shape far better ways of living on the land. Economically, America is rich enough to treat the land with greater respect and to use it in ways that protect its beauty and preserve it for future generations. And lawmakers are adept enough, and have enough flexibility, to craft rules to help bring this about.

Progress, then, depends ultimately on the yearnings of people and on their willingness to imagine different, better ways of inhabiting the land. Organizer Jim McMahon is helping to bring about a new land ethic, and so is farmer and writer Wendell Berry, and so is scientist Wes Jackson, and so are many others all across the country. With enough of them at work—with enough of *us* at work—there is good cause for hope.

Sources, Acknowledgments, and Further Reading

Unlike many books, this one did not begin as a specific project. I can only vaguely date when I began working on it and can only partially acknowledge the sources I used and the many people who aided me along the way. The subjects covered here have occupied my attention for years, and the book arose as much from an attempt to organize my thoughts as from an endeavor to say anything to others. Over the years, I've grabbed hold of ideas that struck me as sound, constantly adding, weeding out, and reformulating in an attempt to imagine how people might live better on the land and with one another. Book writing became a matter of organizing my intellectual and spiritual inventory.

In various ways, small and large, I have been aided in my work by many people, including Donna Becker, John Davidson, Holly Doremus, John Gilpin, Bruce Hannon, Peter Landres, Greg McIsaac, Robert McKim, Curt Meine, David Orr, Jack Paxton, Carol Rose, Mark Sagoff, and Joseph Sax. I am grateful to them for their help, particularly those who challenged what I had to say. Clark Bullard, Jim McMahon, Rob Moore, and Kevin

Proescholdt provided useful information about their own work; in each case, however, the summaries I offer here represent my own interpretations. Wendell Berry and Wes Jackson were particularly generous in taking time not just to talk with me but also to show me their respective homes. Portions of chapters 1 and 5 first appeared in *Stewardship Across Boundaries* (Washington, D.C.: Island Press, 1998). Richard L. Knight and Peter B. Landres, editors of the volume, provided useful comments that helped me clarify my thinking. Portions of chapters 2 and 3 first appeared in an essay prepared for the Program for the Study of Cultural Values and Ethics at the University of Illinois, Urbana-Champaign. Professor Walter Feinberg headed the program at the time, and I thank him for encouraging me to bring together my ideas on the ethical elements of environmental law. That essay in turn was reprinted by the *University of Illinois Law Review* and by the *Environment and Land Use Law Review*. Portions of chapter 3 are also based on a talk I gave in 1996 at the annual conference of the Society for Business Ethics in Quebec; Laura Westra kindly invited me to speak and helped give direction to my thoughts. A version of that talk was published as "Consumption and the Practice of Land Health" in *The Business of Consumption* (Lanham, Md.: Rowman & Littlefield, 1998), edited by Laura Westra and Patricia H. Werhane. Chapter 4 began as an essay titled "Local Value," published in *Terra Nova: Nature & Culture* in 1996; it appears here in much-revised form. An early version of chapter 6 was delivered as a paper at the biennial conference of the American Society for Environmental History in Baltimore in April 1997. Carolyn Merchant arranged the session at which I spoke, and my paper built on her fine work on narratives of property ownership. Carol Rose commented on my talk, giving me ideas that helped improve the piece. I delivered a more law-oriented version of the talk in February 1998 at the Florida State University College of Law, which was published in the fall of 1998, with extensive footnotes, in the *Journal of Land Use & Environmental Law*. Finally, I first brought together ideas in several of the chapters in an essay on environmental thought, "Illinois Life: An Environmental Testament," written at the request of the Illinois Environmental Council for use in its education efforts. With more extensive notes, that essay was reprinted by the *University of Illinois Law Review*. I thank the editors of these various publications for giving me the chance to try out ideas and for offering useful comments.

On the following pages are some of the major sources I used in writing this book, together with the origins of quotations. Although I've benefited from the work of many authors, I've turned to five of them with such regularity that they deserve special mention. Three appear in this book by name—Aldo Leopold, Wendell Berry, and Wes Jackson. Leopold stands as the preeminent conservation writer in American history; *A Sand County Almanac*, as Wallace Stegner put it, is one of our civilization's "prophetic books, the utterance of an American Isaiah" (Wallace Stegner, "The Legacy of Aldo Leopold," in J. Baird Callicott, ed., *Companion to A Sand County Almanac* [Madison: University of Wisconsin Press, 1987], p. 233). Wendell Berry's books, some three dozen in number so far, together provide a vivid, inspiring, humbling portrait of the many ways, good and bad, that people can live on the land. So wide ranging is his thought, and so thoroughly has it influenced me, that I have little idea where his thinking ends and my own begins. My initial attempt at drawing on his work appeared as "The Dilemma of Wendell Berry," *University of Illinois Law Review*, 1994, no. 2 (1994): 363–385. That same feeling of indebtedness, I know, is experienced by many other people, including Berry's good friend Wes Jackson, whose Land Institute at Salina, Kansas, stands as a conservationist's City on the Hill. Jackson's influence stems mostly from his research work and the thinking that goes into it, but his own wide-ranging writings, cited in the section on chapter 8, have been quite helpful to me and others. Two other writers whose work has proven indispensable are historian Donald Worster and philosopher J. Baird Callicott. Both are prolific interdisciplinary scholars at the forefront of conservation thought. So greatly has their work influenced me that it deserves citation in every chapter.

Finally, my thanks go to my editor, Laurie Burnham, whose support, patience, and editing pencil brought this book to life. Even though the project had no starting date, she insisted that it have an ending, and she usefully pushed me to keep things simple.

CHAPTER I

"Mending Wall" appears in Edward Connery Lathem, ed., *The Poetry of Robert Frost* (New York: Holt, Rinehart and Winston, 1969), pp. 33–34. Warren's quote is from Robert Penn Warren, "The Themes of Robert Frost," in his *New and Selected Essays* (New York: Random House, 1989), p.

287. The Supreme Court of California's decision in the Spring Creek dispute is reported as *Tartar v. The Spring Creek Water and Mining Co.*, 5 Cal. 396 (1855). The early history of California water law and water development is considered in Norris Hundley, *The Great Thirst: Californians and Water, 1770s–1990s* (Berkeley: University of California Press, 1992); Mark T. Kanazawa, "Efficiency in Western Water Law: The Development of the California Doctrine, 1850–1911," *Journal of Legal Studies* 27 (1998): 159–184; and Eric T. Freyfogle, "*Lux v. Haggin* and the Common Law Burdens of Modern Water Law," *University of Colorado Law Review* 57 (1986): 485–525. A good case study of the various ways that western settlers inhabited the land is Dean L. May, *Three Frontiers: Family, Land, and Society in the American West, 1850–1900* (Cambridge, England: Cambridge University Press, 1994). The specific setting of irrigation communities is considered in Donald Worster, *Rivers of Empire: Water, Aridity, and the Growth of the American West* (New York: Pantheon Books, 1985), and the general utilitarian slant of western settlement is finely presented in Patricia Nelson Limerick, *The Legacy of Conquest: The Unbroken Past of the American West* (New York: Norton, 1987). The symbolic importance of the frontier is the focus of Henry Nash Smith's classic work *Virgin Land: The American West As Symbol and Myth* (Cambridge, Mass.: Harvard University Press, 1950).

The human drive to control land is considered from a sociological perspective in Robert David Sack, *Human Territoriality: Its Theory and History* (Cambridge, England: Cambridge University Press, 1986). On the rectangular grid land survey process, see Hildegard Binder Johnson, *Order upon the Land: The U.S. Rectangular Land Survey and the Upper Mississippi Country* (New York: Oxford University Press, 1976); a provocative conservation perspective is Curt Meine, "Inherit the Grid," in Joan Iverson Nassauer, ed., *Placing Nature: Culture and Landscape Ecology* (Washington, D.C.: Island Press, 1997). The difficulties of dividing nature into distinct ownership pieces is explored in Theodore Steinberg, *Slide Mountain, or the Folly of Owning Nature* (Berkeley: University of California Press, 1995). The issues that arise in land-management efforts that transcend boundaries are considered in Richard L. Knight and Peter B. Landres, *Stewardship Across Boundaries* (Washington, D.C.: Island Press, 1998). The history of the American environmental movement is considered in Philip Shabecoff, *A Fierce Green Fire: The American Environmental Movement* (New York: Hill & Wang, 1993); Robert Gottlieb, *Forcing the Spring: The Transformation of the American Environmental Movement* (Washington, D.C.: Island Press, 1993); and Kirkpatrick Sale, *The Green Revolution: The American Environmental Movement, 1962–1992* (New York: Hill & Wang, 1993). Many of the dominant ideas of environmentalism are considered in Roderick Frazier Nash, *The Rights of Nature: A History of Environmental Ethics* (Madison: University of Wisconsin Press, 1989), and Bryan G. Norton, *Toward Unity Among Environmentalists* (New York: Oxford University Press, 1991).

CHAPTER 2

Environmental thought in the United States since the 1960s is considered in the books by Shabecoff, Gottlieb, Sale, Nash, and Norton cited in the section on chapter 1. A thoughtful presentation of radical environmental thought is Christopher Manes, *Green Rage: Radical Environmentalism and the Unmaking of Civilization* (Boston: Little, Brown, 1990); a broader consideration is Carolyn Merchant, *Radical Ecology: The Search for a Livable World* (New York: Routledge, 1992). A journalistic study of the radical group Earth First! is Susan Zakin, *Coyotes and Town Dogs: Earth First! and the Environmental Movement* (New York: Penguin Books, 1993). The U.S. Supreme Court's decision in the snail darter case is reported as *Tennessee Valley Authority v. Hill*, 437 U.S. 153 (1978); the snail darter controversy, both before and after the decision, is considered in Zygmunt J. B. Plater, Robert H. Abrams, and William Goldfarb, *Environmental Law and Policy: Nature, Law, and Society* (Minneapolis: West, 1992), pp. 656–673. The Clayton Williams controversy is reported at *Clajon Production Corp. v. Petera*, 854 F. Supp. 843 (D. Wyo. 1994) (the quotation is on p. 846), *aff'd*, 70 F.3d 1566 (10th Cir. 1995). Editorial quotations appear in June Rain, "Wyoming Lawsuit Would Privatize Wildlife," *High Country News*, February 21, 1994, p. 15. Additional information about the controversy was obtained through conversations with staff members of the Wyoming Wildlife Federation, Cheyenne, Wyoming. The U.S. Supreme Court's endorsement of state ownership was made in *Geer v. Connecticut*, 161 U.S. 519, 529 (1896); the decision in *Collopy v. Wildlife Commission, Colorado*, appears at 625 P.2d 994 (1981). Wildlife law is surveyed in Thomas A. Lund,

American Wildlife Law (Berkeley: University of California Press, 1980), and Michael J. Bean and Melanie J. Rowland, *The Evolution of National Wildlife Law*, 3rd ed. (Westport, Conn.: Praeger, 1997).

Legal decisions in the Boundary Waters controversy are reported as *County of St. Louis v. Thomas*, 162 F.R.D. 583 (D. Minn. 1995), and *County of St. Louis v. Thomas*, 967 F. Supp. 370 (D. Minn. 1997). Background on the Boundary Waters controversy is set forth in David Backes, *Canoe Country: An Embattled Wilderness* (Minocqua, Wis.: NorthWord Press, 1991); David Backes, *A Wilderness Within: The Life of Sigurd Olson* (Minneapolis: University of Minnesota Press, 1997); and R. Newell Searle, *Saving Quetico-Superior: A Land Set Apart* (Minneapolis: Minnesota Historical Society, 1979). More recent information appears in the various quarterly issues of *BWCA Wilderness News*, published by the Friends of the Boundary Waters Wilderness. The litigation before the Illinois Pollution Control Board in the Middle Fork of the Vermilion River case was docketed as AS 92-7; the decision was handed down on October 7, 1993. The unpublished opinion of the Appellate Court of Illinois for the Fourth District, enrolled as No. 4-93-0959, was issued on September 8, 1994.

A good place to enter the diverse field of environmental philosophy, in addition to sources already cited, is Michael E. Zimmerman et al., *Environmental Philosophy: From Animal Rights to Radical Ecology*, 2nd ed. (Upper Saddle River, N.J.: Prentice Hall, 1998). Two particularly good personal syntheses are Lester W. Milbrath, *Envisioning a Sustainable Society: Learning Our Way Out* (Albany: State University of New York Press, 1989), and Mitchell Thomashow, *Ecological Identity: Becoming a Reflective Environmentalist* (Cambridge, Mass.: MIT Press, 1995). An indispensable survey of ecological thought in the United States is Donald Worster, *Nature's Economy: A History of Ecological Ideas*, 2nd ed. (Cambridge, England: Cambridge University Press, 1994). Two leading works on the ethical status of individual animals are Tom Regan, *The Case for Animal Rights* (Berkeley: University of California Press, 1983), and Peter Singer, *Animal Liberation*, rev. ed. (New York: Avon Books, 1990). The differences between ethical schemes based on animal rights and those based on community values are considered in Eugene C. Hargrove, ed., *The Animal Rights/ Environmental Ethics Debate: The Environmental Perspective* (Albany: State University of New York Press, 1992). The Berry quote is from Wendell

Berry, *The Long Legged House* (New York: Harcourt, Brace & Co., 1969) p. 77. The Leopold quote is from Aldo Leopold, *A Sand County Almanac, and Sketches Here and There* (New York: Oxford University Press, 1949), pp. 224–225.

CHAPTER 3

The most manageable survey of federal environmental law is William Rodgers, *Environmental Law* (St. Paul, Minn.: West, 1994, 1998 update). NEPA is now codified at 42 U.S.C. §§ 4321–4370d (1994) (quotations are from § 4331). One observer not misled by NEPA was Joseph Sax, who anticipated its limitations in his article "The (Unhappy) Truth About NEPA," *Oklahoma Law Review* 26 (1973): 239–248. The Multiple-Use Sustained-Yield Act is codified at 16 U.S.C. §§ 528–531 (1994); quotations are from § 531. The ocean dumping quotation is from 33 U.S.C. § 1401(b) (1994); the Clean Air Act quotation is from 42 U.S.C. § 7602(4) (1994); the Clean Water Act quotation is from 33 U.S.C. § 1251(a) (1994). Implementation of the Clean Water Act is critically assessed in Robert W. Adler, Jessica C. Landman, and Diane M. Cameron, *The Clean Water Act Twenty Years Later* (Washington, D.C.: Island Press, 1993). The Wilderness Act is now codified at 16 U.S.C. §§ 1131–1136 (1994); its legal background is considered in Michael McCloskey, "The Wilderness Act of 1964: Its Background and Meaning," *Oregon Law Review* 45 (1966): 288–321; the quotation is from 16 U.S.C. § 1131(a). The Endangered Species Act is codified at 16 U.S.C. §§ 1531–1544 (1994); quotations are from §§ 1531(b) and 1533(b)(2). The statute is summarized in Michael J. Bean and Melanie J. Rowland, *The Evolution of National Wildlife Law*, 3rd ed. (Westport, Conn.: Praeger, 1997). Its implementation is critically assessed in Oliver A. Houck, "The Endangered Species Act and Its Implementation by the U.S. Departments of Interior and Commerce," *University of Colorado Law Review* 64 (1993): 277–370. The listing process is carefully examined in Holly Doremus, "Listing Decisions Under the Endangered Species Act: Why Better Science Isn't Always Better Policy," *Washington University Law Quarterly* 75 (1997): 1029–1153. One of Congress's unsuccessful efforts to address private land-use issues is assessed in Corwin W. Johnson and Valerie M. Fogelman, "The Farmland Protection Policy Act: Stillbirth of a Policy?" *University of Illinois Law Review*

1986 (1986): 581–607. Its problems in remedying polluted runoff from private lands are reviewed in Daniel R. Mandelker, "Controlling Non-point Source Water Pollution: Can It Be Done?" *Chicago-Kent Law Review* 65 (1989): 479–502. A good inquiry into the shift of environmental policy away from the pollution model is Donald T. Hornstein, "Lessons from Federal Pesticide Regulation on the Paradigms and Politics of Environmental Law Reform," *Yale Journal of Law and Regulation* 10 (1993): 369–446.

Aldo Leopold's ideas are expressed not just in his classic *A Sand County Almanac* (see the section on chapter 2) but also in his *Round River: From the Journals of Aldo Leopold* (New York: Oxford University Press, 1953) and in a fine collection of his shorter works, *The River of the Mother of God and Other Essays by Aldo Leopold*, ed. J. Baird Callicott and Susan L. Flader (Madison: University of Wisconsin Press, 1991). The Leopold quotation is from *Round River*, pp. 146–147. An excellent biography of Leopold is Curt Meine, *Aldo Leopold: His Life and Work* (Madison: University of Wisconsin Press, 1988). Leopold's land ethic is ably considered in J. Baird Callicott, *In Defense of the Land Ethic: Essays in Environmental Philosophy* (Albany: State University of New York Press, 1989); a perceptive earlier study is Susan L. Flader, *Thinking Like a Mountain: Aldo Leopold and the Evolution of an Ecological Attitude Toward Deer, Wolves, and Forests* (Columbia: University of Missouri Press, 1974). Callicott is today the leading proponent of a holistic land ethic that draws on Leopold's work; a recent essay of his, responding to current ideas in ecological thought, is "Do Deconstructive Ecology and Sociobiology Undermine Leopold's Land Ethic?" *Environmental Ethics* 18 (1996): 353–372. Callicott considers Leopold's vision of land health in his "Aldo Leopold's Metaphor," in Robert Costanza, Bryan G. Norton, and Benjamin D. Haskell, eds., *Ecosystem Health: New Goals for Environmental Management* (Washington, D.C.: Island Press, 1992), pp. 42–56. Leopold's thought is also usefully assessed in J. Baird Callicott, ed., *Companion to A Sand County Almanac* (Madison: University of Wisconsin Press, 1987), and Thomas Tanner, ed., *Aldo Leopold: The Man and His Legacy* (Ankeny, Iowa: Soil Conservation Society of America, 1987). Criticisms of Leopold's ethic are reviewed in Eric T. Freyfogle, "The Land Ethic and Pilgrim Leopold," *University of Colorado Law Review* 61 (1990): 217–256.

Ecosystem health as an environmental policy goal is assessed from various perspectives in Robert Costanza, Bryan G. Norton, and Benjamin D. Haskell, eds., *Ecosystem Health: New Goals for Environmental Management* (Washington, D.C.: Island Press, 1992). The related idea of ecological integrity is considered in Laura Westra and John Lemons, eds., *Perspectives in Ecological Integrity* (Dordrecht, Netherlands: Kluwer, 1995), and in Laura Westra, *An Environmental Proposal for Ethics: The Principle of Integrity* (Lanham, Md.: Rowman & Littlefield, 1994). Sustainable development as an international environmental policy goal is presented in World Commission on Environment and Development, *Our Common Future* (New York: Oxford University Press, 1987). An American example is National Commission on the Environment, *Choosing a Sustainable Future* (Washington, D.C.: Island Press, 1993). Numerous, widely varied interpretations of sustainability are compared in Richard P. Gale and Sheila M. Cordray, "Making Sense of Sustainability: Nine Anwers to 'What Should Be Sustained?'" *Rural Sociology* 59 (1994): 311–332. A more ecologically responsive interpretation of sustainability is presented in J. Baird Callicott, "The Wilderness Idea Revisited: The Sustainable Development Alternative," in Christopher Key Chapple, ed., *Ecological Prospects* (Albany: State University of New York Press, 1994), pp. 37–63. A thoughtful, comprehensive synthesis is Lester W. Milbrath, *Envisioning a Sustainable Society: Learning Our Way Out* (Albany: State University of New York Press, 1989).

In addition to sources cited in the sections on chapters 1 and 2, the ethical aspects of land health are considered in Bryan G. Norton, ed., *The Preservation of Species: The Value of Ecological Diversity* (Princeton, N.J.: Princeton University Press, 1986); Bryan G. Norton, *Why Preserve Natural Variety?* (Princeton, N.J.: Princeton University Press, 1987); and Annette Baier, "For the Sake of Future Generations," in Tom Regan, ed., *Earthbound: New Introductory Essays in Environmental Ethics* (Philadelphia: Temple University Press, 1984), pp. 214–246. Religious dimensions are surveyed in John E. Carroll, Paul Brockelman, and Mary Westfall, eds., *The Greening of Faith: God, The Environment, and the Good Life* (Hanover, N.H.: University Press of New England, 1997), and Robert Booth Fowler, *The Greening of Protestant Thought* (Chapel Hill: University of North Carolina Press, 1995).

A leading consideration of the unruliness of natural communities in terms of constituent species is Daniel B. Botkin, *Discordant Harmonies: A New Ecology for the Twenty-First Century* (New York: Oxford University Press, 1990). Two useful assessments are Michael Barbour, "Ecological Fragmentation in the Fifties," in William Cronon, ed., *Uncommon Ground: Toward Reinventing Nature* (New York: Norton, 1995), pp. 233–255, and S. T. A. Pickett and Richard S. Ostfield, "The Shifting Paradigm in Ecology," in Richard L. Knight and Sarah F. Bates, eds., *A New Century for Natural Resources Management* (Washington, D.C.: Island Press, 1995), pp. 261–278. Two texts on the theory of ecology are Kristen S. Shrader-Frechette and Earl D. McCoy, *Method in Ecology: Strategies for Conservation* (Cambridge, England: Cambridge University Press, 1993), and Stuart L. Pimm, *The Balance of Nature? Ecological Issues in the Conservation of Species and Communities* (Chicago: University of Chicago Press, 1991). A detailed survey of the literature is included in Mark Sagoff, "Muddle or Muddle Through? Takings Jurisprudence Meets the Endangered Species Act," *William and Mary Law Review* 38 (1997): 825–993. Donald Worster, the leading historian of ecological thought, puts current trends in perspective in his *Nature's Economy: A History of Ecological Ideas*, 2nd ed. (Cambridge, England: Cambridge University Press, 1994), especially part VI. My discussion of sources of the renewed emphasis on change in natural communities draws heavily on that work and on Donald Worster, "The Ecology of Order and Chaos," in his *Wealth of Nature: Environmental History and the Ecological Imagination* (New York: Oxford University Press, 1993), pp. 156–170. The "is/ought" distinction is considered in an environmental context in J. Baird Callicott, "Hume's *Is/Ought* Dichotomy and the Relation of Ecology to Leopold's Land Ethic," in J. Baird Callicott, ed., *In Defense of the Land Ethic: Essays in Environmental Philosophy* (Madison: University of Wisconsin Press, 1989), pp. 117–127. The Leopold quote ("integrity, stability, and beauty") is from pp. 224–225 of *A Sand County Almanac*. Leopold's essay on *Draba* appears on p. 26 of *A Sand County Almanac*.

CHAPTER 4

The reasons for liberalism's prominence in America are considered in Louis Hartz, *The Liberal Tradition in America* (New York: Harcourt, Brace & World, 1955). Hartz's analysis remains useful, although he has been criticized for exaggerating the political consensus that emerged from that tradition. A lucid presentation and defense of liberalism, highlighting its focus on the individual, is John Gray, *Liberalism* (Minneapolis: University of Minnesota Press, 1986). Liberalism's roots in the early nineteenth century are considered in Lawrence Frederick Kohl, *The Politics of Individualism* (New York: Oxford University Press, 1989). A prominent libertarian text, focused on the individual as property owner and on the discreteness of land parcels, is Richard A. Epstein, *Takings: Private Property and the Power of Eminent Domain* (Cambridge, Mass.: Harvard University Press, 1985). Two penetrating critiques of the human-centeredness and excessive rationalism of modern thought are David Ehrenfeld, *The Arrogance of Humanism* (New York: Oxford University Press, 1978), and John Ralson Saul, *Voltaire's Bastards: The Dictatorship of Reason in the West* (New York: Free Press, 1992). How these ideas altered the Western understanding of nature is considered in Carolyn Merchant, *The Death of Nature* (New York: Harper & Row, 1980).

The critique of individualism in social terms is also at the center of the growing body of literature on communitarianism. Amitai Etzioni is a leading figure, and all his work can be usefully consulted, though it has little to say directly about the land community. His most recent work is *The New Golden Rule: Community and Morality in a Democratic Society* (New York: Basic Books, 1996). A highly useful collection of essays, comparing communitarian and liberal thought and highlighting the ethical assumptions that originally underlay liberal thought, is Amitai Etzioni, ed., *New Communitarian Thinking: Persons, Virtues, Institutions, and Communities* (Charlottesville: University of Virginia Press, 1995); another good comparison is Stephen Mulhall and Adam Swift, *Liberals and Communitarians* (Cambridge, Mass.: Blackwell, 1992). A particularly pointed critique of individualism is Willard Gaylin and Bruce Jennings, *The Perversion of Autonomy: The Proper Uses of Coercion and Constraints in Liberal Society* (New York: Free Press, 1996). A reformulation from a political perspective is Michael J. Sandel, *Democracy's Discontent: America in Search of Public Philosophy* (Cambridge, Mass.: Harvard University Press, 1996). A more sociological perspective is presented in Robert N. Bellah et al., *Habits of the Heart: Individualism and Commitment in American Life* (Berkeley: University of California Press, 1985).

Wendell Berry stands as the most eloquent advocate for a more holistic view of people and land; the entire body of his work can be usefully consulted on the issues covered in chapter 4 of this book. Citations to his work are set forth in the section on chapter 5. Wes Jackson's contributions include his *Becoming Native to This Place* (Lexington: University of Kentucky Press, 1985). The writing of Scott Russell Sanders is particularly eloquent on the need to sink roots; his work includes *Staying Put: Making a Home in a Restless World* (Boston: Beacon Press, 1993) and *Writing from the Center* (Bloomington: Indiana University Press, 1995). An excellent recent addition to this literature is Alan Thein Durning, *This Place on Earth: Home and the Practice of Permanence* (Seattle: Sasquatch Books, 1996). A classic expression of bioregionalism as an orientation toward the land is Kirkpatrick Sale, *Dwellers in the Land: The Bioregional Vision* (San Francisco: Sierra Club Books, 1985). An ecological critique of economic thought is set forth in Herman E. Daly and John B. Cobb Jr., *For the Common Good: Redirecting the Economy Toward Community, the Environment, and a Sustainable Future* (Boston: Beacon Press, 1989). On the possibilities of land management that transcends boundaries, see Richard L. Knight and Peter B. Landres, eds., *Stewardship Across Boundaries* (Washington, D.C.: Island Press, 1998).

The judicial decision in the *Alger* case appears as *Commonwealth v. Alger*, 7 Cush. 53 (Mass. 1851); the quotations are from pp. 84–85. The New York judicial quotation is from V*anderbilt v. Adams*, 7 Cow. 349 (1827), pp. 351–352. The idea of a well-ordered society is considered in William J. Novak, *The People's Welfare: Law and Regulation in Nineteenth-Century America* (Chapel Hill: University of North Carolina Press, 1996), and Gregory S. Alexander, *Commodity and Propriety: Competing Visions of Property in American Legal Thought, 1776–1970* (Chicago: University of Chicago Press, 1997).

CHAPTER 5

"The Boundary" appears in Wendell Berry's short story collection *The Wild Birds* (San Francisco: North Point Press, 1986), pp. 75–98; the quotations are from pp. 96–97. Useful essays on Berry's work appear in Paul Merchant, ed., *Wendell Berry* (Lewiston, Idaho: Confluence Press, 1991). The leading study is Andrew J. Angyal, *Wendell Berry* (New York: Twayne, 1995), which contains a good bibliography (pp. 163–173) of both Berry's writings and secondary literature. The importance of local community is a dominant theme of Berry's work. Important expressions of this theme include "The Work of Local Culture," in *What Are People For?* (San Francisco: North Point Press, 1990), pp. 153–169; "People, Land, and Community," in *Standing By Words* (San Francisco: North Point Press, 1983), pp. 64–79; and "Conservation and Local Economy" and "Conservation Is Good Work," from his *Sex, Economy, Freedom, and Community* (New York: Pantheon Books, 1993), pp. 3–18, 27–43. A clear expression of Berry's views of the way people and nature fit together is his "Getting Along with Nature," in his *Home Economics* (San Francisco: North Point Press, 1987), pp. 6–20. The Berry quotations on property are from "Whose Head Is the Farmer Using? Whose Head Is Using the Farmer?" in Wes Jackson, Wendell Berry, and Bruce Colman, eds. *Meeting the Expectations of the Land* (San Francisco: North Point Press, 1984), p. 30.

No scholar has yet undertaken a study of Berry's influence on contemporary conservation thought, nor has an effort been made to explore how Berry has transformed southern agrarian thought.

CHAPTER 6

Wallace Stegner's novel *The Big Rock Candy Mountain* was first published by Doubleday & Company in 1943. Stegner's ideas and influence are considered in Curt Meine, ed., *Wallace Stegner and the Continental Vision: Essays on Literature, History, and Landscape* (Washington, D.C.: Island Press, 1997), and Charles E. Rankin, ed., *Wallace Stegner: Man and Writer* (Albuquerque: University of New Mexico Press, 1996).

The visions and utopian dreams of American colonists provide an organizing focus in Daniel J. Boorstin, *The Americans: The Colonial Experience* (New York: Random House, 1958). A classic study of Winthrop's mission is Edmund S. Morgan, *The Puritan Dilemma: The Story of John Winthrop* (Boston: Little, Brown, 1958). Various Christian interpretations of the Garden of Eden story are presented in Elaine Pagels, *Adam, Eve, and the Serpent* (New York: Random House, 1988). My discussion of the conflicting Eden narratives in America draws heavily on Donald Worster, *The Wealth of Nature: Environmental History and the Ecological Imagination* (New York: Oxford University Press, 1993), pp. 9–15; Carolyn Merchant, "Reinventing Eden: Western Culture as a Recovery Narrative," in

William Cronon, ed., *Uncommon Ground: Toward Reinventing Nature* (New York: Norton, 1995), pp. 132–159; and Carolyn Merchant, "Paradise and Property: Locke's Narrative and the Transformation of Nature" (unpublished paper, 1997). An illustrative contemporary use of Eden as a goal for modern culture in its land relations is Ian Bradley, *God Is Green: Ecology for Christians* (New York: Image Books, 1990), p. 65. Sources on the rise of individualism in America and the emergence of a market economy, in addition to those cited in the section on chapter 4, include Allan Kulikoff, *The Agrarian Origins of American Capitalism* (Chapel Hill: University of North Carolina Press, 1992), and J. E. Crowley, *This Sheba, Self: The Conceptualization of Economic Life in Eighteenth-Century America* (Baltimore: Johns Hopkins University Press, 1974).

Locke's theory of private property rights is presented largely in his "Second Treatise of Government"; see John Locke, *Two Treatises of Government*, ed. Peter Laslett (Cambridge, England: Cambridge University Press, 1988). Locke's theory is ably critiqued in Lawrence G. Becker, *Property Rights: Philosophic Foundations* (London: Routledge, 1977), and fit into the history of property ownership ideas in Richard Schlatter, *Private Property: The History of an Idea* (London: Russell & Russell, 1973). Ideas of property ownership in America are surveyed in William B. Scott, *In Pursuit of Happiness: American Conceptions of Property from the Seventeenth Century to the Twentieth Century* (Bloomington: Indiana University Press, 1977); a detailed consideration focused more on legal context is Gregory S. Alexander, *Commodity and Propriety: Competing Visions of Property in American Legal Thought, 1776–1970* (Chicago: University of Chicago Press, 1997). Useful considerations of the role of narratives in debates over private property include Carol M. Rose, "Property As Storytelling: Perspectives from Game Theory, Narrative Theory, Feminist Theory," *Yale Journal of Law and the Humanities* 2 (1990): 37–57, and Myrl Duncan, "Property As a Public Conversation, Not a Lockean Soliloquy: A Role for Intellectual and Legal History in Takings Analysis," *Environmental Law* 26 (1996): 1095–1160. Jefferson's ideas appear principally in his *Notes on the State of Virginia*, which is portrayed as a defense of the perfection of nature in America in chapter 4 of Roderick Nash, *Wilderness and the American Mind*, 3rd ed. (New Haven, Conn.: Yale University Press, 1982), and as a pastoral ideal in Leo Marx, *The Machine in the Garden: Technology and the Pastoral Ideal in America* (New York: Oxford University Press, 1984). Nash's book also considers the late-nineteenth-century interest in the outdoors and in conservation, as does Samuel P. Hays, *Conservation and the Gospel of Efficiency: The Progressive Conservation Movement, 1890–1920* (Cambridge, Mass.: Harvard University Press, 1959).

Richard Epstein's ideas appear principally in his book *Takings: Private Property and the Power of Eminent Domain* (Cambridge, Mass.: Harvard University Press, 1985), though he has also written dozens of articles on the subject, including "Possession As the Root of Title," *Georgia Law Review* 13 (1979): 1221–1243, where he presents in greatest detail his argument in favor of first occupancy as the means of gaining ownership and critiques Locke's labor theory. Other important statements by him include "A Clear View of the Cathedral: The Dominance of Property Rules," *Yale Law Journal* 106 (1997): 2091–2120; "*Lucas v. South Carolina Coastal Council:* A Tangled Web of Expectations," *Stanford Law Review* 45 (1993): 1369–1392; and "Property As a Fundamental Civil Right," *California Western Law Review* 29 (1992): 187–207. Also useful is his article "The Static Conception of the Common Law," *Journal of Legal Studies* 9 (1980): 253–289. Epstein's reworking of Locke occurs principally on pp. 9–12 of *Takings*. A recent expression of the libertarian view of property rights, couched as a defense of the institution, is Nancie G. Marzulla and Roger G. Marzulla, *Property Rights: Understanding Government Takings and Environmental Regulation* (Rockville, Md.: Government Institutes, 1997).

Justice Scalia's ideas are surveyed in two articles by Fred Bosselman, "Scalia on Land," in David Callies, ed., *After Lucas: Land Use Regulation and the Taking of Property Without Compensation* (Chicago: American Bar Association, 1993), pp. 82–101, and "Four Land Ethics," *Environmental Law* 24 (1994): 1439–1511. The decision in *Nollan v. California Coastal Commission* is at 483 U.S. 825 (1987); the decision in *Lucas v. South Carolina Coastal Council* appears at 505 U.S. 1003 (1992); the decision in *Babbitt v. Sweet Home Chapter* is at 515 U.S. 687 (1995), with Justice Scalia's dissenting opinion beginning at p. 714. Additional decisions that reveal Justice Scalia's reasoning include *Suitum v. Tahoe Regional Planning Agency*, 117 S. Ct. 1659, 1670 (Scalia, J., dissenting); *Stevens v. City of Cannon Beach*, 510 U.S. 1207 (1994) (Scalia, J., dissenting from denial of certiorari), and *Lujan v. Defenders of Wildlife*, 504 U.S. 555 (1992). The "historical compact" quotation is from *Lucas*, 505 U.S. 1028. The dissenting opinions in *Lucas*, by Justices Harry A. Blackmun and John P. Stevens, appear at 505 U.S. 1036 (Blackmun, J., dissenting) and 505 U.S. 1061 (Stevens, J., dissenting).

The view of private property ownership as an evolving communal creation is expressed lucidly in Joseph William Singer and Jack M. Beerman, "The Social Origins of Property," *Canadian Journal of Law and Jurisprudence* 6 (1993): 217–248. Singer, a leading proponent of this view, addresses other aspects in "No Right to Exclude: Public Accommodations and Private Property," *Northwestern University Law Review* 90 (1996): 1283–1495; "Sovereignty and Property," *Northwestern University Law Review* 86 (1991): 1–56; and "The Reliance Interest in Property," *Stanford Law Review* 40 (1988): 611–751. Joseph Sax, another law professor, is an equally prominent proponent of this perspective. His extensive writings include "Property Rights and the Economy of Nature: Understanding *Lucas v. South Carolina Coastal Council*," *Stanford Law Review* 45 (1993): 1433–1455, and "Some Thoughts on the Decline of Private Property," *Washington Law Review* 58 (1983): 481–496. Other useful works include Myrl Duncan's article, cited earlier in this section; Lynda L. Butler, "Private Land Use, Changing Public Values, and Notions of Relativity," *Brigham Young University Law Review* 1992 (1992): 629–667; and T. Nicolaus Tideman, "Takings, Moral Evolution, and Justice," *Columbia Law Review* 88 (1988): 1714–1730. Leopold's comments on property ownership appear principally in his *A Sand County Almanac* and *Round River*, as noted in the sections on chapters 2 and 3, respectively, but many appear in less accessible essays and letters. One illustration of the various ways in which property rights can be crafted is William Cronon, *Changes in the Land: Indians, Colonists, and the Ecology of New England* (New York: Hill & Wang, 1983), which examines seventeenth-century Algonquian practices in New England. The leading study of long-term communal property arrangements is Elinor Ostrom, *Governing the Commons: The Evolution of Institutions for Collective Action* (Cambridge, England: Cambridge University Press, 1990). A fine introduction to the growing body of scholarship criticizing traditional landownership norms as ecologically unsound is Terry Frazier, "The Green Alternative to Classical Liberal Property Theory," *Vermont Law Review* 20 (1996): 299–371. The Wisconsin decision in *Just v. Marinette County* appears at 201 N.W.2d 761 (1972); the quotations are from p. 768.

No full study of Edward Abbey's thought yet exists. His life is recounted in James Bishop Jr., *Epitaph for a Desert Anarchist: The Life and Legacy of Edward Abbey* (New York: Atheneum, 1994). Much of Abbey's work is considered in Ann Ronald, *The New West of Edward Abbey* (Albuquerque: University of New Mexico Press, 1982). The Abbey quotation is from his *Desert Solitaire: A Season in the Wilderness* (New York: Ballantine Books, 1971), p. 185.

CHAPTER 7

Robert Frost's poem appears in Edward Connery Lathem, ed., *The Poetry of Robert Frost* (New York: Holt, Rinehart and Winston, 1969), p. 1. Berry's poem is in *A Part* (San Francisco: North Point Press, 1980), p. 3. As does chapter 5, this chapter draws widely on the work of Wendell Berry. See the section on chapter 4 for sources regarding the value of community and the need to sink roots. Berry's work is often autobiographical; particularly useful are the various writings in his *Recollected Essays, 1965–1990* (San Francisco: North Point Press, 1981). Additional useful sources are William Vitek and Wes Jackson, eds., *Rooted in the Land: Essays on Community and Place* (New Haven, Conn.: Yale University Press, 1996); Hildegarde Hannum, ed., *People, Land, and Community* (New Haven, Conn.: Yale University Press, 1997); and Stephanie Mills, *In the Service of the Wild: Restoring and Reinhabiting Damaged Land* (Boston: Beacon Press, 1995). A foundational source for all such assessments is, of course, Thoreau's *Walden*, which is perceptively considered in the context of environmental thought in Lawrence Buell, *The Environmental Imagination: Thoreau, Nature Writing, and the Formation of American Culture* (Cambridge, Mass.: Harvard University Press, 1995). My criticisms of global thinking and of the moral implications of free trade borrow heavily from the writings of Wendell Berry, particularly "Out of Your Car, Off Your Horse" and "A Bad Big Idea" from his *Sex, Economy, Freedom, and Community* (New York: Pantheon Books, 1993), pp. 19–26, 45–51. The differing roles of individuals as citizens and consumers are discussed in Mark Sagoff, *The Economy of the Earth: Philosophy, Law, and the Environment* (New York: Oxford University Press, 1988).

CHAPTER 8

Wes Jackson's ideas are set forth in his *New Roots for Agriculture*, new ed. (Lincoln: University of Nebraska Press, 1985); *Altars of Unhewn Stone* (San Francisco: North Point Press, 1987); and *Becoming Native to This Place* (Lexington: University of Kentucky Press, 1994). Two Land Institute staff members provide more scientific detail of their methods in Judith D. Soule and Jon K. Piper, *Farming in Nature's Image: An Ecological Approach to Agriculture* (Washington, D.C.: Island Press, 1992). That work is usefully supplemented by Maria R. Finckh and Martine S. Wolfe, "The Use of Biodiversity to Restrict Plant Diseases and Some Consequences for Farmers and Society," in Louise E. Jackson, ed., *Ecology and Agriculture* (San Diego: Academic Press, 1997), pp. 203–237, and in the same volume, Matt Liebman and Eric R. Gallandt, "Many Little Hammers: Ecological Management of Crop-Weed Interactions," pp. 291–343. The idea of turning to nature for guidance is poetically expressed by Wendell Berry in "Nature As Measure," in his *What Are People For?* (San Francisco: North Point Press, 1990), pp. 204–210. A particularly pointed critique of modern farming is Berry's *The Unsettling of America: Culture and Agriculture* (San Francisco: Sierra Club Books, 1977). Other useful assessments, with proposals for change, are Marty Strange, *Family Farming: A New Economic Vision* (Lincoln: University of Nebraska Press, 1988); Gregory McIsaac and William R. Edwards, eds., *Sustainable Agriculture in the American Midwest: Lessons from the Past, Prospects for the Future* (Urbana: University of Illinois Press, 1994); National Research Council, *Alternative Agriculture* (Washington, D.C.: National Academy Press, 1989); Trauger M. Groh and Steven S. McFadden, *Farms of Tomorrow: Community Supported Farms, Farm Supported Communities* (Kimberton, Pa.: Bio-Dynamic Literature, 1990); Gene Logsdon, *At Nature's Pace: Farming and the American Dream* (New York: Pantheon Books, 1994); and William Lockeretz, ed., *Visions of American Agriculture* (Ames: Iowa State University Press, 1997). The mimetic tradition is considered in Carolyn Merchant, "Restoration and Reunion with Nature," in Bill Willers, ed., *Learning to Listen to the Land* (Washington, D.C.: Island Press, 1991), pp. 206–211.

In addition to the sources cited in the section on chapter 6, good materials on the reformulation of private landownership norms include Timothy Beatley, *Ethical Land Use: Principles of Policy and Planning* (Baltimore:

Johns Hopkins University Press, 1994), and Lynton K. Caldwell and Kristen Shrader-Frechette, *Policy for Land: Law and Ethics* (Lanham, Md.: Rowman & Littlefield, 1993). I express views on the takings issue in "The Owning and Taking of Sensitive Lands," *UCLA Law Review* 43 (1995): 77–138, and discuss the beneficial-use requirement in water law in "Water Rights and the Common Wealth," *Environmental Law* 26 (1996): 27–51. Joseph Sax considers the historical roots of the public trust doctrine in "The Public Trust Doctrine in Natural Resources Law: Effective Judicial Intervention," *Michigan Law Review* 68 (1970): 471–566, and describes a possible future in "Liberating the Public Trust Doctrine from Its Historical Shackles," *University of California Davis Law Review* 14 (1980): 185–194. The Supreme Court quotation is from *Mugler v. Kansas*, 123 U.S. 623, 665 (1887). The quotations from Justinian are from *Justinian's Institutes*, book 2, title 1, part 1.

CHAPTER 9

Land-use planning on the watershed or ecosystem level is considered in many sources, including W. William Weeks, *Beyond the Ark: Tools for an Ecosystem Approach to Conservation* (Washington, D.C.: Island Press, 1997); Fred B. Samson and Fritz L. Knopf, eds., *Ecosystem Management: Selected Readings* (New York: Springer-Verlag, 1996); Steven L. Yaffee et al., *Ecosystem Management in the United States: An Assessment of Current Experience* (Washington, D.C.: Island Press, 1996); and Richard Haeuber, "Setting the Environmental Policy Agenda: The Case of Ecosystem Management," *Natural Resources Journal* 36 (1996): 1–28. An excellent survey of the literature on ecosystem management, distilling the shared elements of various proposals, is R. Edward Grumbine, "What Is Ecosystem Management?" *Conservation Biology* 8 (March 1994): 27–38. Some of the legal challenges are considered in Robert Adler, "Addressing the Barriers to Watershed Protection," *Environmental Law* 25 (1995): 973–1106, and Lee Breckenridge, "Reweaving the Landscape: The Institutional Challenge of Ecosystem Management for Lands in Private Ownership," *Vermont. Law Review* 19 (1995): 363–422. The challenges of integrating science into public policy decision making are considered in Kai N. Lee, *Compass and Gyroscope: Integrating Science and Politics for the Environment* (Washington, D.C.: Island Press, 1993). Proposals for practical implementation are presented in Timothy Beatley and Kristy Manning, *The Ecology of Place: Planning for Environment, Economy, and Community* (Washington, D.C.: Island Press, 1997), and Eve Endicott, ed., *Land Conservation Through Public/Private Partnerships* (Washington, D.C.: Island Press, 1993).

No book has been more influential in promoting a rethinking of government processes for dealing with citizens than Daniel Kemmis, *Community and the Politics of Place* (Norman: University of Oklahoma Press, 1990), from which I have drawn in my critique of government hearing processes and on other points. Also useful is DeWitt John, *Civic Environmentalism: Alternatives to Regulation in States and Communities* (Washington, D.C.: Congressional Quarterly Press, 1994), and Benjamin Barber, *Strong Democracy: Participatory Politics for a New Age* (Berkeley: University of California Press, 1984).

CODA

The Leopold quote in the epigraph is from p. 41 of *A Sand County Almanac*, as cited in the section on chapter 2. The quotations from Willa Cather's *My Ántonia* (Boston: Houghton Mifflin, 1918) are from pp. 14–16, and 18. The quote by Oliver Wendell Holmes is from a letter quoted in James Woodress, *Willa Cather: A Literary Life* (Lincoln: University of Nebraska Press, 1987), p. 302.

Index

Abbey, Edward, 110–12
Abolitionism, 64
Activists, environmental, 19
Adam and Eve in the Garden of Eden, 93–94, 96
Aesthetic appeal of rivers, 157, 162–63
A. G. Chauncey & Co., 7–11, 146–47, 168, 169
Agriculture:
   agrarian alternative to modern ways of interpreting and dwelling on the land, 82–86, 159
   farming methods, 86, 116
   imitating nature, 134–36
   Land Institute, 131–34
   monocultures, 118, 132
   polyculture of perennial species, 133
   soil erosion, 132, 158
   stewardship duties, 123
   See also Staying home
Agriculture, U.S. Department of, 155–56
Air pollution, 18
Alger, Cyrus, 73

American Farm Bureau Federation, 143, 156
Animals, humans viewed as the only important, 31–33, 52–53
Animals wisely using the land, 135
Anthropocentrism, 31
Appalachia Science in the Public Interest, 159
Assessments, data-bound environmental, 34–35

Balance of nature, 58
Beachfront property rights, 103–4
Beauty, land as an object of, 79
Bees, 56
Behavior, informal standards of, 124–25
Beneficial use, doctrine of, 145–47
Berry, Wendell:
   community efforts to promote land health, 167
   conversing with the land, 135–36
   dependence on the Earth, 36
   land ethic, a new, 176

Individual rights, 64
Informal standards of behavior,
124–25
Informal voluntary mechanisms, 87
Information-based approach exemplified by NEPA, 42
Information clearinghouse for land-use
ideas, local community as a,
123–24
Institutes (Justinian), 146
Institutional support for new land
ethic, 159
Interconnections, ecological, xv, 17, 21
ecology, popular wisdom of, 13–14
environmental disputes, recurring
concern in, 31
global thinking, 121–22
goal of land health, 48–49
hunting and property rights/wildlife
laws, 36
ills, environmental, 40
Mackinaw River, 163–65
Mat Feltner's world, 81–82
Intergenerational asset, farm as, 123
International trade laws, 122
Isolation, decisions in, 128–29

Jackson, Wes, 131, 133–34, 136, 150,
159–60, 176
Jefferson, Thomas, 95, 160
Justinian, 146

Kentucky, 83, 117, 149–50
See also Mat Feltner's world
Knowledge:
limits of human, 33–35
local, handing down of, 84
special knowledge about a given
place, 79

Labor, property rights arriving out of,
99–100
Labor adding value to the land,
human, 102
Labor and individualistic view of the
world, 66
Land:
beauty, as an object of, 79

conversing with the, 135–36
human advancement and valuing, 32
inattentiveness to land's natural fea-
tures/processes, 81
individualistic view of the world,
66–69
past, staying home and understanding land's, 117–18
regulations for use of, 112–13, 129
restoration, landscape-level, 14
tallgrass prairie, 131–34
See also Property rights
Land ethic:
balance of nature, 58
community-oriented, 37
creating a new, steps to take in,
174–75
excellence, pursuing, 145
health, land, 51–54, 158
imagination, 176
institutional support, 159
Mat Feltner's world, 81
shifting, 96
worldwide acceptance of concept,
58–59
Land health:
altering practices, 151
collective goal, 59
community participation, 16,
129–30, 167
creek in Champaign-Urbana (IL),
61–63
ethics of, 51–54, 81, 96, 158
goal needed to explain conservation,
clear and specific, 48–51, 175
government, state and federal,
165–67
imitating nature, 134–36
individualistic view of the world,
71–72
new perspective on landownership,
crafting a, 109–10
obstacles to cooperative promotion
of, 59
scientific side of, 54–58
See also Mackinaw River; Staying
home
Land Institute, 131–35, 159